09|10

The Press Photographer's Year

The Press Photographer's Year would like to thank all the photographers who submitted photographs for the competition and for kindly allowing us to reproduce them in this book and at the accompanying exhibition.

The copyright for each of the photographs published in this book is held by the individual photographer, with the exception of the following publications and agencies:

The Press Photographer's Year are very grateful to them for their permissions.

Agence France Presse; 48, 66, 73 top, 92
Associated Press; 77 top
BBC; 36
Brighton Evening Argus; 22 bottom
Clare People; 44 both
Daily Mail; 24 all, 25, 39, 69 bottom, 89 bottom, 110
Getty Images; 22 top, 26, 38, 41 bottom, 42, 56 top, 57 bottom, 71, 76, 78, 82 top, 85, 88, 102, 104, 106, 108, 109 both, 113, 116 both, 117, 118
The Guardian; 9, 10, 18 bottom, 29, 55
The Independent; 90 bottom
Manchester Evening News; 84
Maverick; 53 top
Pacemaker Press; 33 top
Photocall Ireland; 80
Press Association; 19 top, 32, 58, 59, 67, 77 bottom, 90 top, 91
Reuters; 114
Scotland on Sunday; 33 bottom
South West News Service; 51 bottom, 57 top
Swindon Advertiser; 105
The Sun; 112
UPPA; 111

All the copyright holders have asserted their moral rights under the UK Copyright Designs & Patents Act 1988.

The Press Photographer's Year would not have been possible without the generous support of Canon Cameras. We would like to thank Matt Beard at Canon UK for his dedication to the project.

We would also like to thank the following people for their time, their support and valuable assistance during The Press Photographer's Year.

2009 Jury
Brian Harris (Chairman)
Roger Hutchings
Terry Richards
Homer Sykes
Neil Turner

2009 Sports Jury
Bob Martin (Chairman)
Russell Cheyne

at TalkingPixels.co.uk
Tom Scott, James Crossett, Zbyszek Zemla

at SMITH
Stuart Smith, Victoria Forrest, Selina Swayne, Namkwan Cho

at the National Theatre
John Langley, Alison Chown, Caroline Ansdell

at Passavia, Passau
Elmar Steubl, Michael Wallrapp, Sandra Kössl

at Loxley Colour, Glasgow
Christopher Kay, Robert Orr, Audrey Smith

a special vote of thanks must go to
Alastair Mackeown
Nigel Learmond & Brian Murphy

thanks also to
Hazel Dunlop, Stuart Morcom, Victoria Routledge, Allan Titmuss,

A major exhibition of the photographs from this book was held at the National Theatre on London's South Bank between 4th July and 31st August 2009 and was designed by SMITH, printed by Loxley Colour and sponsored by Canon.

Published by the PPY PRESS
Press Photographers Year Ltd.
47 Moore Park Road
London SW6 2HP
call us: +44(0)20 3239 9908
email us: info@theppy.com
visit us: www.theppy.com

Produced by Dillon Bryden & Tim Bishop
Collated by Dillon Bryden & Neil Turner
Design: SMITH, Victoria Forrest, Selina Swayne
www.smith-design.com

Printing & Repro: Passavia, Passau

Printed in Germany on Profi Silk 170 gsm and Invercote G 300 gsm acid-free papers.

ISBN 978-0-9556019-2-7

09

The Press Photographer's Year

Following spread
Photograph of the Year
Rosie Hallam
Thirteen orphaned elephants are looked after around the clock by a team of dedicated carers at the David Sheldrick Elephant Orphanage, Nairobi, Kenya. Elephants who lose their family are very hard to care for. They often die of a broken heart. At the David Sheldrick Orphanage they have devised a system of care which involves sleeping, eating and being with the young elephants all the time. This gives them a much greater chance of survival. The carers find it hard not to get attached to the baby elephants who are constantly craving affection. 11th January 2009

Foreword
Brian Harris
Chairman of the 2009 Jury

A staff photographer for The Times before being appointed Chief Photographer of the Independent before its launch in 1986, Brian's strong visual style contributed to the newspaper's reputation as one of the most admired 'picture papers' in the world. This is his reflection on the 2009 awards.

UK and Ireland based press photographers, editorial photographers, operators, photojournalists, togs, snappers, smudgers, monkeys and many other forms of nomenclature far too impolite to write here have over the past century produced some of the greatest 'news photography' in the world.

The selection in this book represents a continuation of that great tradition. But with the advent of editorial cutbacks across the entire industry, will that tradition survive? Many major newspapers have fired most of their staff and contract photographers, relying instead on photo-agencies and freelance contributors who are being offered terms of far less value than a decade ago. Some reproduction fees have fallen to less than a pint of beer. In short, the editorial photography business is in crisis: from an economic perspective, it's borderline unsustainable.

It is my opinion that the majority of newspapers have lost a major part of their individuality by diluting their own very specific visual identity, as they use more and more outsourced material - imagery that has to serve many different masters.

It appears that their visual journalistic commitment has been diminished, maybe a contributing factor to the massive decline in the number of newspapers being sold over the past decade.

All of the above makes our edit here all the more remarkable. In the face of these adverse market conditions great images can still be produced. If nothing else, your average 'press snapper' is a dogged old soul who does not give up - that's what makes us good at our job! Diligence coupled with belligerence.

Our task, viewing over 7,800 submitted images, firstly projected onto a screen in a small darkened room, then as photographic prints, made for a rather intensive ten-hour no-holds-barred way of finding a set of winning entries. After a couple of hours a fellow juror asked the question, 'Where's the picture?' We all agreed that although we were seeing a lot of photography, we were not actually seeing that many great photographs. We worked out that this could be one of the potentially negative side-effects of the digital revolution. Far too many images, all perfectly sharp and correctly exposed, but somehow saying less. The bar of technical quality had certainly been raised in the middle ground but has the intellectual bar actually been raised at the very top level?

As Chair I decided that we would have a mantra to work from. Our winning pictures should have to be 'Great pictures of relatively ordinary events rather than ordinary pictures of great events'.

We started to look at the images differently. It was what the image said and how it was composed within the rectangle that became our guiding light, rather than the actual event depicted. Images away from the London beat started to filter towards the top of the pile - there was freshness, a raw honesty within the imagery that started to shine through.

I have always maintained that a good photographer should be able to make a humdinger of a picture in his or her garden if only they bothered to look. Sadly, many photographers don't get their toys out of the bag until the phone rings and they have a commission. In these straitened times many photographers are wondering if their phone actually still works! Making great images isn't just about getting on a plane and jetting off to exotic parts: quite often it's about engaging with your local community and documenting the ordinary in a stimulating, aesthetically pleasing way, wherever you live.

With these thoughts in mind we were pleased to award First Prize: Photo Essay to Manchester based Bruce Adams of the Daily Mail for his superb and sensitive coverage of the harrowing Shannon Matthews missing schoolgirl story. Jeff Overs, who works for the BBC, produced a charming seen juxtaposition with his image of a jogger passing Battersea Power station; and both Eamon Ward and Graham Trott produced sensitive observations of 'Clare People' and 'Cider Makers' respectively. All were local stories to each photographer.

Irina Kalashnikova's beautifully photographed coverage of life in North Korea was a perfect example of what passes for normality in that part of the world, while closer to home Laurence Griffiths produced a simple but evocative picture of a family playing cricket on the beach in the West Country.

Adrian Dennis and Roger Bamber both made me smile with their respective takes on a 'Naked Bike Run' and 'Children reflected in a Hall of Mirrors': once again small situations but brilliantly observed.

Even at a 'big' news event, a great photographer can produce subtle imagery such as Peter Macdiarmid's picture of Amy Winehouse waiting to hear if she had won an award.

Although Rosie Hallam's beautiful picture was made overseas at the Elephant Orphanage in Kenya, we on the jury voted overwhelmingly in favour of awarding her the Photograph of the Year award. This picture struck a chord with us all, it has vibrancy, it is positive and it has life... It is in fact just a Great Picture. Nothing more and nothing less.

Introduction

Tim Bishop
Co-founder of The Press Photographer's Year

I've found that many people who work in press photography have been reciting that great cliché: 'it's when things get tough, that you find out who your friends really are'. Fellow photographers competing over less and less work, picture editors juggling anorexic budgets, and favours begged to help out on projects that need the kind of hard work and input that simply can't be bought.

The Press Photographer's Year is just such a project. It relies heavily on tough friends. And this last two years, the friends have had to get very tough indeed.

Let me just remind you of the brief: we'd like to produce an exhibition of some of the finest press photography in the world, we'd like to hold it at one of the most recognised public landmarks in London, we'd like to show the results as a permanent record in a beautifully designed book, and above all, we want to invite photographers to submit their work in the easiest, fastest way possible, to be judged by their peers, all of whom will be photographers that the entrants themselves will know, respect, whose work they will have admired. Everyone who enters will have their work shown to this jury, not only on screen, but in hard copy as well. And we'll do it bang smack in the middle of a global recession.

You'll find this year's Press Photographers' Year book is in fact two books in one. It represents both the 2009 and 2010 competition entries in one wrap. View the images from 2009, and turn the book over to see 2010. I shudder to imagine the conversations that Matt Beard of Canon UK must have had on our behalf with the leaders of the world's finest camera manufacturer. He secured funding for our exhibition during the recession freeze of 2009, and managed to ring fence enough budget for us in a not much warmer 2010 to produce a bigger, bumper book covering both year's competitions.

All this against a background where newspapers have cut back hugely, in an industry where slashing costs have been part of the scene for years. It's pressure forcing a dramatic change in press photography. The dwindling numbers of photographers that do still work directly for newspapers find that they are paid, in real terms, considerably less than they were just a decade ago, and hugely less than twenty years ago. They find they are competing with the rise of the photographic agencies, previously seen by many as an apprenticeship before joining a great newspaper, but now relied upon by the picture desks as the dominant source of news coverage.

So the next cliché: 'Tough times don't last, but tough friends do'. And the PPY has a ring of tough friends, not least John Langley and his assistant Alison Chown at the National Theatre, their commitment a keystone of the PPY. Thanks too to Chris Kay and his team at Loxley, our exhibition printers, who rise to the challenge each year

with an eye blinkingly fast turn around. Tom Scott, James Crossett and Zbyszek Zemla of Talking Pixels, who built and maintain our ground breaking website, making this the most 'entrant friendly' competition for news photographers based in the UK. Hold on, change that, it's now the only competition for news photographers in the UK.

We are indebted to our distinguished panels of jurors who waded through over 7,500 entries for both the 2009 and 2010 awards. They gave freely of their time to sit hunched in dark rooms watching slide show after slide show before assembling under the tall glass 'cathedral windows' of our hosts the National Theatre, to discuss, debate, and pick the edit and winners from hard copy prints laid out painstakingly over the carpet.

The 2009 jury was led by Chairman, Brian Harris, and featured Homer Sykes, Roger Hutchings, Neil Turner, Terry Richards, Russell Cheyne, and Bob Martin. The 2010 jury was Chaired by Roger Allen and was comprised of Nic Dunlop, Neil Turner, Jez Coulson, Graham Trott, and Rosie Hallam, with the sport judged by Chairman, Tom Jenkins, and Stuart MacFarlane, and finally, our 2010 multimedia judging was Chaired by Dan Chung ably supported by Rodney Charters ASC, Dr D J Clark, Kate Pattison and Adam Westbrook.

Stu Smith, Victoria Forrest and Selina Swayne have refreshingly updated the design for our 'double book'. Neil Turner, vice chair of The British Press Photographers' Association, and juror for two consecutive competitions, brought his expertise to help with the production of the book, travelling out to oversee the book printing in Germany. Alistair Mackeown, Nigel Learmond and Brian Murphy have proved vital and longstanding supporters. Tough, tough friends. We owe them all a huge vote of thanks.

Press photography is not in decline, but enduring painful and rapid change, accelerated by digital technology, given fire by declining revenues. This double book chronicles this change through the vision of our co-founder, Dillon Bryden, whose determination keeps the only competition for press photographers by press photographers alive. Hold tight, enjoy the ride through some of the finest news photography in the world.

Adam Dean PANOS
Shi Shi Mo, aged 82, is helped to walk over what is left of destroyed homes in Hanwang, Sichuan province, China, after the devastating earthquake. 20th May 2008

Richard Humphries POLARIS IMAGES
The body of a woman killed after a massive quake lies covered in what was once the city market. A 7.9-magnitude earthquake struck China's Sichuan province on 12th May 2008 Tens of thousands of people remained buried in collapsed buildings, and a death toll of over 69,000 was expected to climb as relief operations spread into the mountains of Sichuan province with well over 130,000 military troops and relief workers mobilised. Caring for tens of thousands of people made homeless across the disaster zone has stretched the government's resources thin. State media reported that 10 million people have been directly affected by the quake. 16th May 2008

Dan Chung THE GUARDIAN
Bodies of those caught in the 12th May earthquake lie in what remains of the Beichuan Middle School, Sichuan Province, China: one of the worst affected places. 1,300 school children and their teachers were killed. 15th May 2008

Following spread
Dan Chung THE GUARDIAN
A rescue worker holds a red flag aloft the rubble of
earthquake hit Beichuan, Sichuan province, China.
The flags became a common site in the days Following
the earthquake, with many rescue teams carrying them
to mark a rallying point in the search for survivors.
17th May 2008

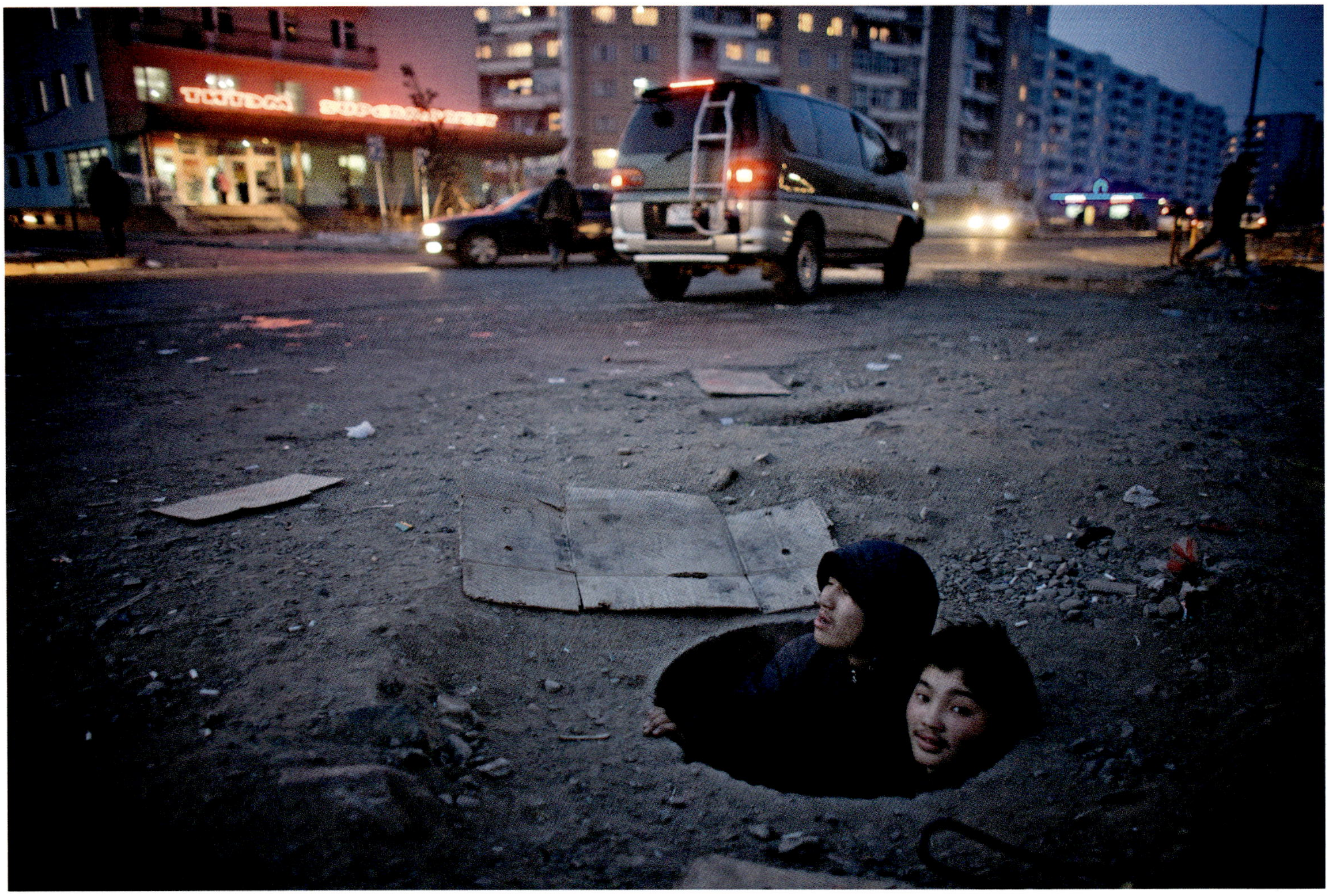

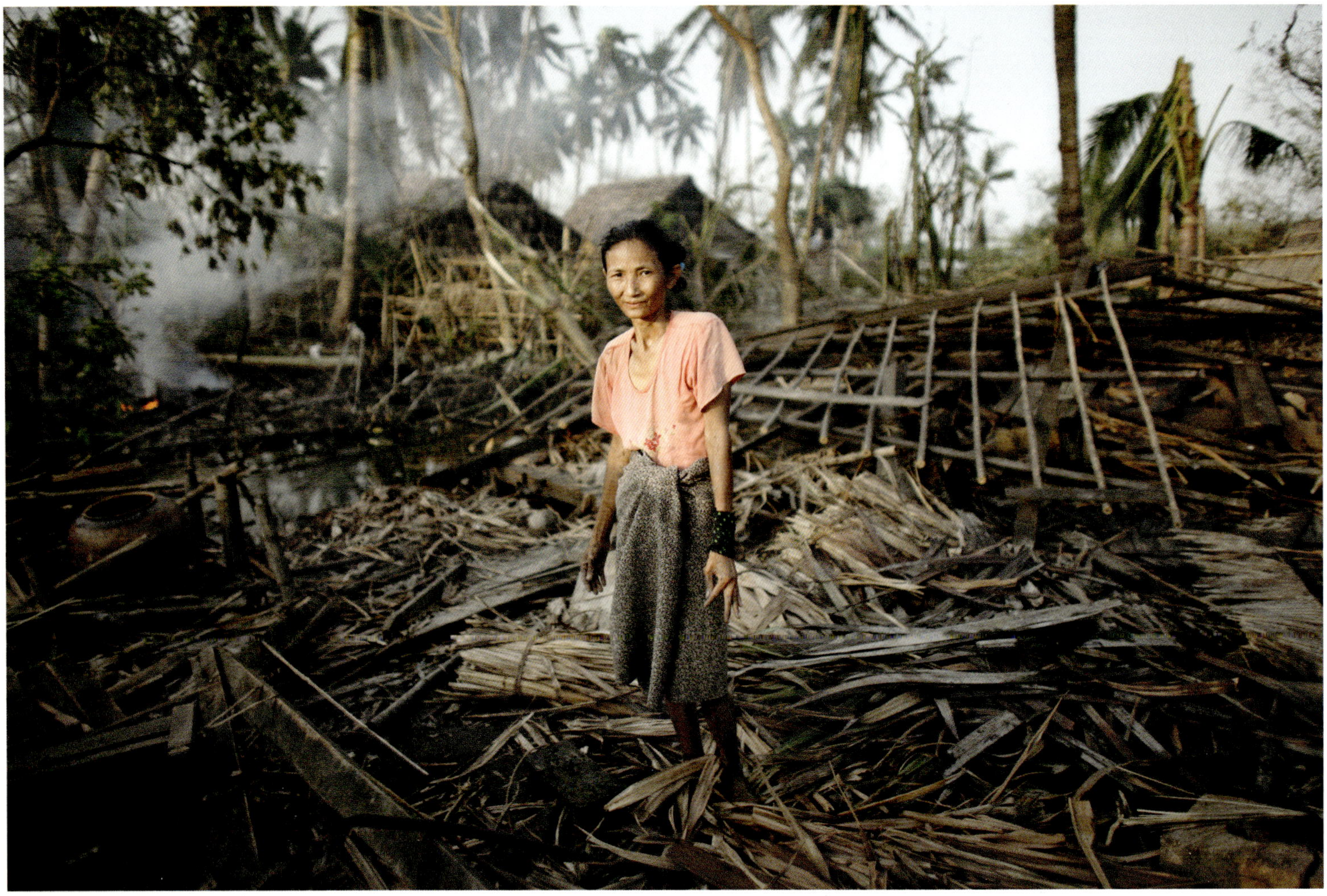

Richard Wainwright
Munkhbat (15) & Altangeret (15) have lived down this manhole in Unur district of Ulaan Baatar for over 3 years. Their daily lives revolve around seeking food and warmth as temperatures drop to minus 40 degrees centigrade. Pipes that provide the city with hot water heat the manholes. It is a tough, lonely existence, where violence from drunken adults and other street children is ever-present. 18th January 2009

Adam Dean PANOS
A woman sifts through the debris of her destroyed home near Kunyangon, Myanmar after Cyclone Nargis passed through, creating winds of up to 250kph. 10th May 2008

Angela Catlin
Gaza under siege. Mohammed Majed, a fisherman, sleeps in the nets of the family business after a night out on the boats. The effects of the blockade were felt most acutely at Gaza's hospitals where dozens of patients endured delayed treatment because of dire shortages of medical supplies. Doctors claimed that 220 people had died as a direct result of Israel's policy. 16th July 2008

Following spread
Andrew McConnell PANOS
The Chefferie IDP site, home to some 4,000 people, in the town of Kitchanga, North Kivu, DR Congo. The camp started to form in October 2007 and as of February 2008 still had not received humanitarian assistance due to the instability of the area. 18th February 2008

Jack Hill THE TIMES

A young girl stands in a market in Khotan, Xinxiang province in the far west of China. The region is inhabited predominantly by the Uigher Muslim group and was recently the scene of violence against the Chinese authority. 3rd August 2008

Following spread

Andrew McConnell PANOS

Displaced children sit outside their makeshift homes in the Mugunga 1 IDP site, home to some 10,000 people, in Goma, North Kivu, DR Congo. 5th February 2008

Sean Smith THE GUARDIAN

A mother mourns for her son who was shot in his house when rebels entered the town of Kiwanja near Rutshuru in DR Congo. 5th November 2008

Julien Behal PRESS ASSOCIATION

Single father Maxwell 'Kallon' Fornah, a striker with the Sierra Leone Amputee Football team and his 5-month-old son Junior in their shack in Aberdeen Amputee camp, Freetown, Sierra Leone. 17th October 2008

Kieran Dodds TEARFUND UK

Children in Gulu, North Uganda recover from the trauma of war with loving support from Noah's Ark charity as they move back into the community. The 20-year conflict in North Uganda between the Lord's Resistance Army (LRA) and the government has destroyed the lives and families of many thousands of people in the region. Children once sheltered at Noah's Ark in Gulu to protect them against abduction by the LRA. Now Noah's Ark offer counselling and support to children coping on their own and dealing with the past trauma and stigma, allowing them to reintegrate into families and communities. 5th March 2008

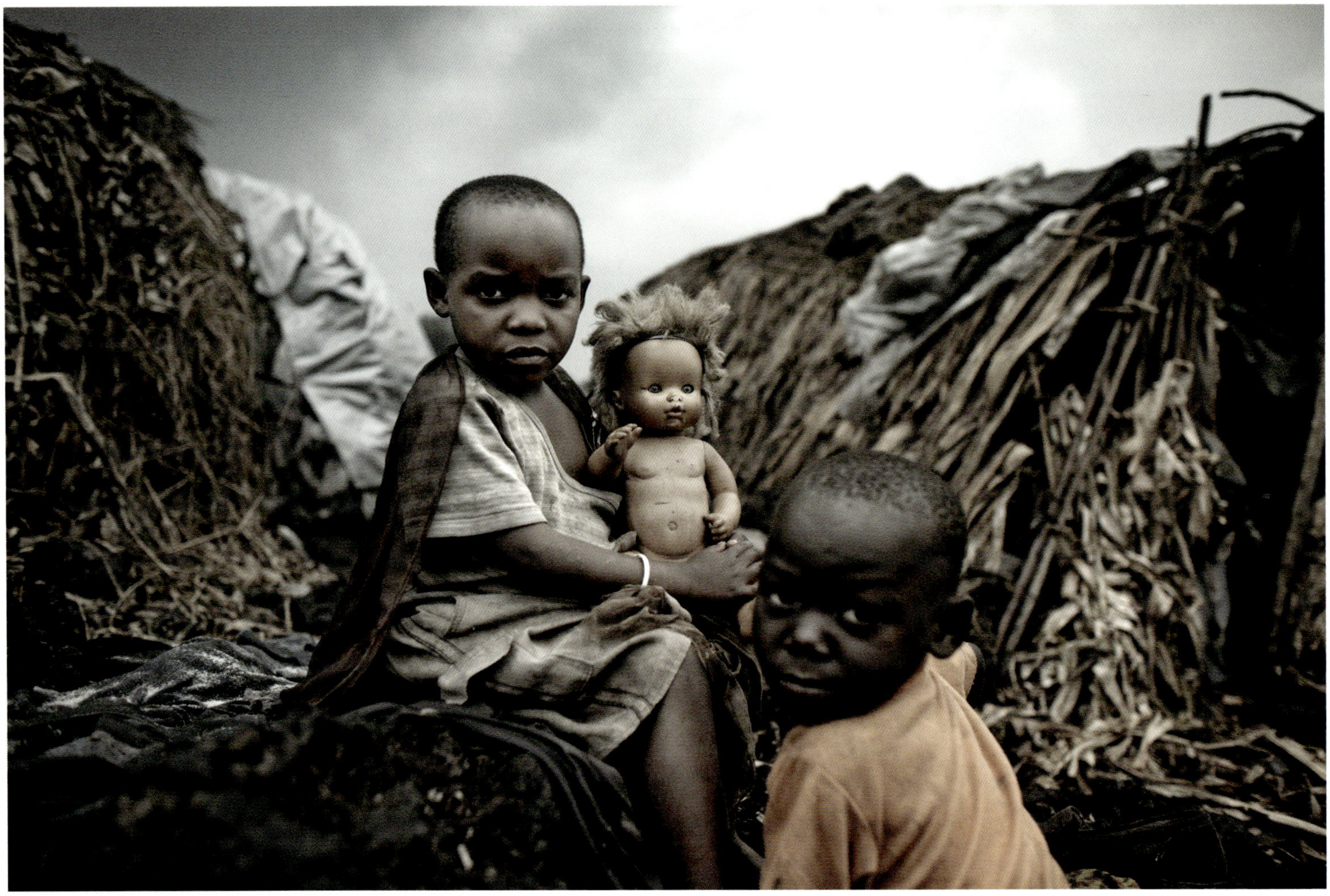

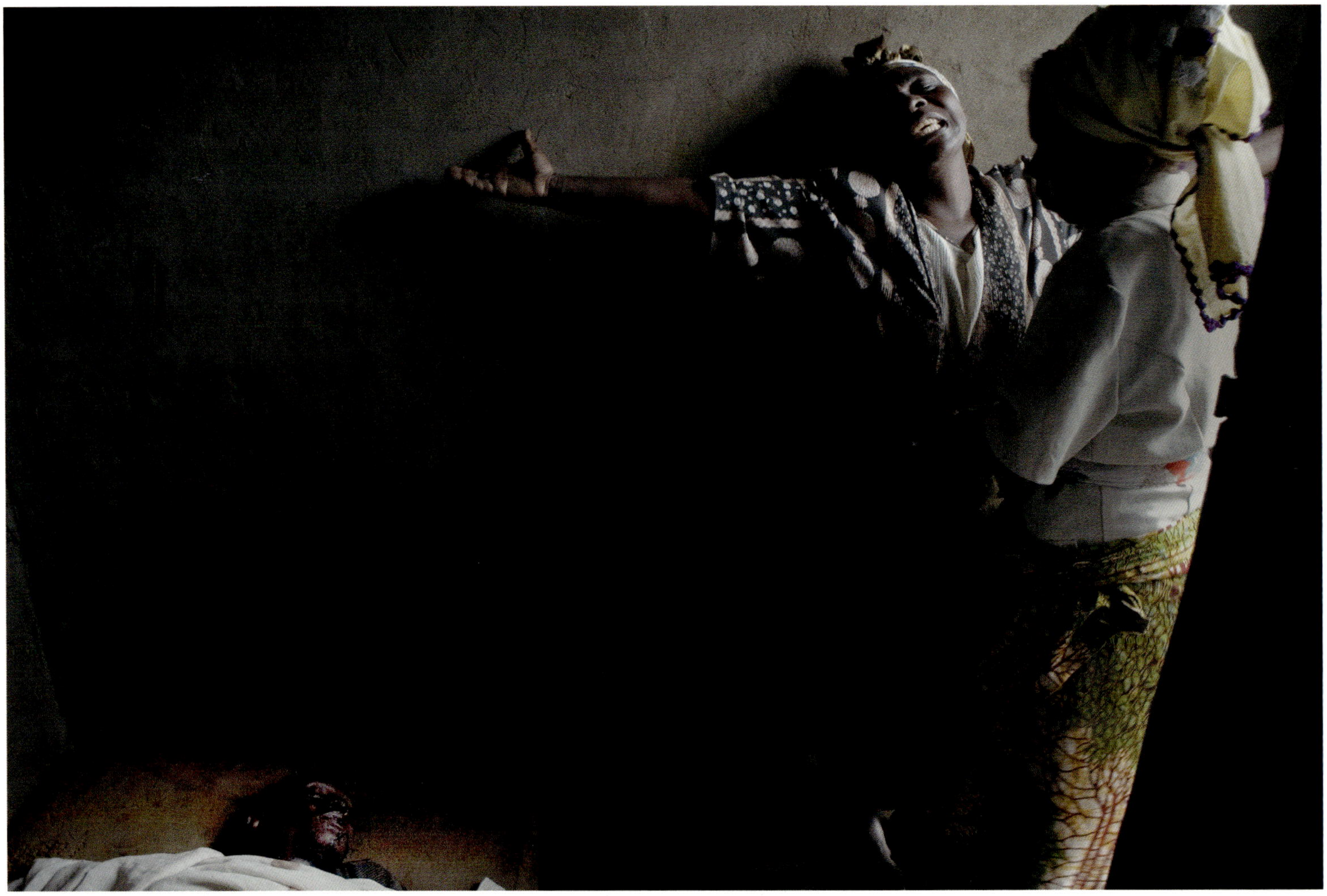

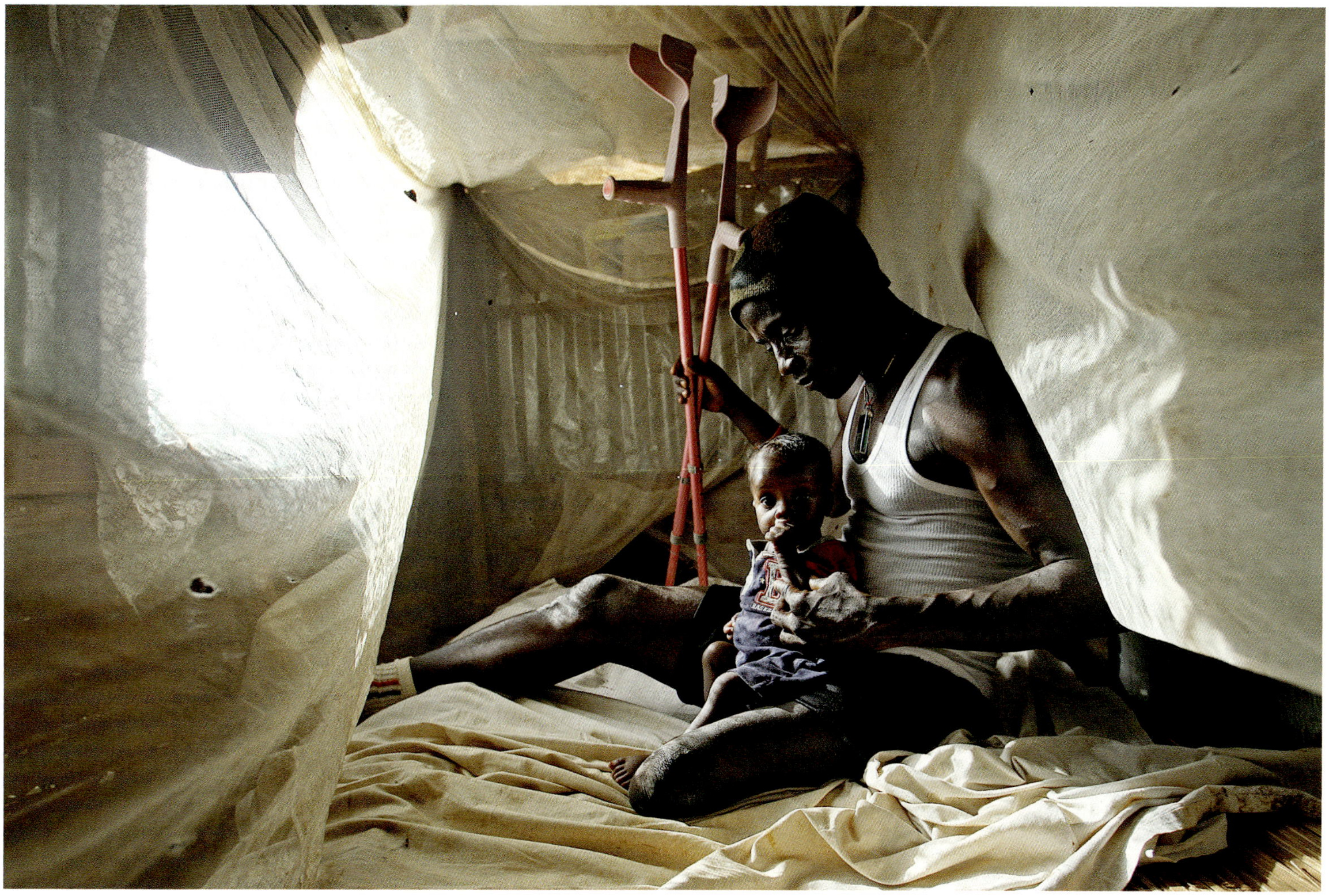

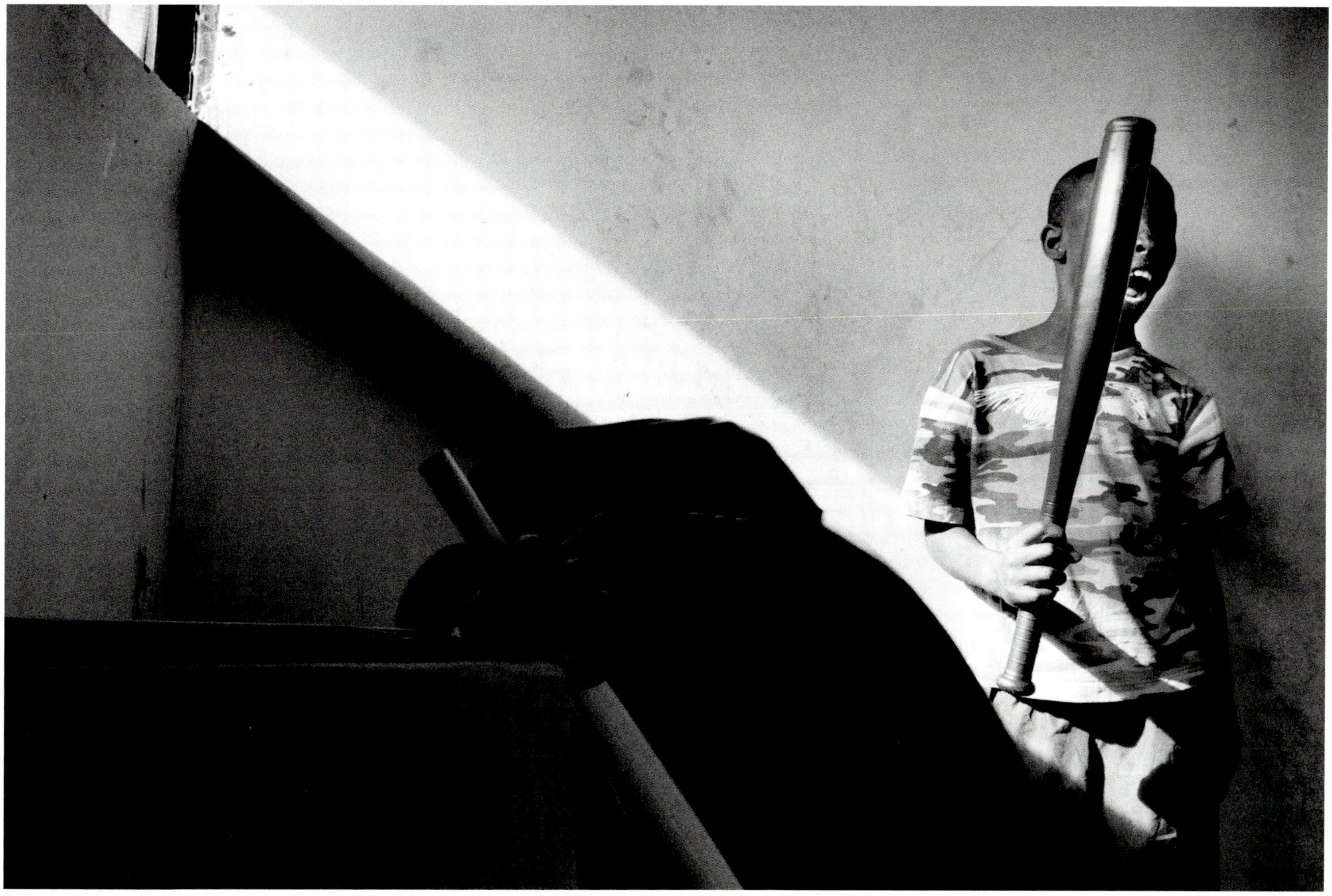

Abbie Trayler-Smith PANOS

Boni, 43, arrived in the UK in March 2005, claiming asylum, and was immediately placed in detention for sixteen weeks at Harmondsworth Immigration Removal Centre. He had been a wealthy businessman in Kinshasa, DR Congo. In 2005 he was arrested and detained on suspicion of opposing president Kabila. While in detention he was forced into an electric chair, was repeatedly beaten and had a knife plunged through his armpit. He was also stabbed from his chest to his groin and his torture scars remain clearly visible. On arrival in the UK Boni was shocked to find himself incarcerated again so soon after escaping from torture in Kinshasa. When he was released from detention he was destitute. He is now receiving section 4 support from the UK Border Agency but for fifteen months survived on almost nothing. The UK government publishes figures of rejected asylum seekers but no statistical breakdown of what happens to them Following the rejection of their claims. This under- ground and invisible population of refused asylum seekers are left completely destitute, prohibited from working and ineligible for welfare support.
9th February 2008

Rosie Hallam

The memorial garden at the St Pancras & Islington cemetery in north London where 'Baby P's' ashes are scattered. 'Baby P' was the alias of a 17-month old boy who died in London after suffering more than 50 injuries over an eight-month period, during which he was repeatedly seen by social services. 'Baby P's' real name was revealed as Peter after the conclusion of a subsequent trial of Peter's mother's boyfriend on a charge of raping a 2-year-old. His mother, her boyfriend, and a second man living with them were all convicted of causing or allowing the death of a child.
26th November 2008

First Prize: News Folio
Peter Macdiarmid GETTY IMAGES
Protestors clash with mounted riot police outside the Israeli embassy in London. Demonstrations and vigils were held all that week as the conflict between Israel and Hamas continued. 10th January 2009

Simon Dack BRIGHTON EVENING ARGUS
Police using batons and pepper spray clashed with 'Smash EDO' protestors on the Lewes Road as they tried to get through to the EDO arms factory in Moulsecoomb near Brighton. 15th October 2008

Jess Hurd REPORTDIGITAL.CO.UK
Protesters are trampled by horses in a clash with riot police outside the Israeli Embassy. National Palestine Demonstration, 'Stop Gaza Massacre' London. 10th January 2009

ROYAL GARDEN HOTEL
Israel out of Gaza
STOP THE SLAUGHTER

WORTHING
POLICE

First Prize: Photo Essay
Bruce Adams DAILY MAIL
A police officer stands guard outside the home of the missing schoolgirl Shannon Matthews as it is illuminated by the lights from TV crews gathered on the Dewsbury Estate, West Yorkshire. 17th March 2008

First Prize: Photo Essay
Bruce Adams DAILY MAIL
Shannon Matthews' mother Karen, and her step-father Craig Meehan on the steps of their home after being told that their daughter had been found alive inside the drawer of a divan base in a nearby flat belonging to Craig Meehan's uncle, Michael Donovan, only a mile from her home. 15th March 2008

First Prize: Photo Essay
Bruce Adams DAILY MAIL
An unknown face stares out from the front window of Shannon Matthews' parents' house in Dewsbury, West Yorkshire. 16th March 2008

First Prize: Photo Essay
Bruce Adams DAILY MAIL
As missing schoolgirl Shannon Matthews is found alive, Chief Constable of West Yorkshire Police, Sir Norman Bettison leaves after giving a statement to the media about the investigation into her disappearance. 17th March 2008

First Prize: Photo Essay
Bruce Adams DAILY MAIL
Shannon Matthews' mother Karen leaves Dewsbury Police Station in West Yorkshire bound for her first appearance at Dewsbury Magistrates Court. 9th April 2008

Following spread
First Prize: Live News
Daniel Berehulak GETTY IMAGES
Party revellers enjoy the atmosphere on the London Underground during a cocktail party on the Circle Line on the last evening that Londoners can consume alcohol on public transport. The cocktail party, organised on the networking website Facebook, attracted thousands of revellers to enjoy one last drink before the ban's enforcement on 1st June. The ban, introduced by the new London Mayor Boris Johnson, is an attempt to clean up unruly behaviour on the London public transport system. 31st May 2008

Stuart Griffiths
Liverpool, England. Teenage kids disgruntled with life and a society that they feel neglects their interests often see no other option than to be a member of a gang. To them, it provides a sense of belonging. A gang member from the 'Nogga Dogz' street gang brandishes a 9mm semi automatic pistol. 16th April 2008

Sean Smith THE GUARDIAN
On the night shift with the police department in Roanoke, Virginia, USA. A young man has been stabbed and collapsed on his porch. 10th October 2008

Following spread
Andrew Testa PANOS
'Convict Poker' at the Angola Maximum Security
Prison in the US. Four inmates sit at a poker table
whilst a bull is released into the arena. The bull is
encouraged to charge the players and the winner
of the game is the prisoner who remains seated the
longest. Angola Maximum Security Prison was at
one time the most violent in the US but has undergone
a transformation under warden Burl Cain who has
expanded the rodeo into an event that attracts over
ten thousand spectators. Whilst it is dismissed by
many as barbaric, others claim the rodeo serves as a
distraction for the prisoners of Angola, 71% of whom
are serving life sentences – which in Louisiana means
that the only way they will leave the prison is in a coffin.
20th April 2008

Anthony Devlin PRESS ASSOCIATION
A sniper surveys the ground from the roof of the stadium during the first England v. India Test Match at the M. A. Chidambaram Stadium in Chennai, India. 11th December 2008

Charles McQuillan PACEMAKER PRESS
Major Shove Gilby reflects on the loss of members and close friends from his battalion after returning from duty in Helmand province, Afghanistan. Palace Barracks, Belfast. 18th June 2008

Phil Wilkinson SCOTLAND ON SUNDAY
A soldier signals to the pilot of a British Lynx helicopter as it lands at the Forward Operating Base 'Edinburgh' near Musa Qala, Afghanistan which had just been captured by British and Afghan forces. 15th February 2008

Eddie Mulholland THE DAILY TELEGRAPH

The Royal Air Force Red Arrows fly in formation with four Typhoon aircraft over central London. The flypast marks the start of a year of events commemorating the formation of the RAF in 1918. 1st April 2008

Following spread
First Prize: Features
Jeff Overs BBC
A jogger runs past Battersea Power Station in south
London. 14th July 2008

Paul Gilham GETTY IMAGES
Competitors race away from the start on the 17.3
kilometre circuit during the Enduropale race, featuring
over one thousand motorbikes in the 4th Enduropale
du Touquet 2009 at Le Touquet Beach in France.
22nd February 2009

Bruce Adams DAILY MAIL
The Seatruck vessel MS Riverdance runs aground on
Anchorsholme beach, Cleveleys, north of Blackpool
after it is hit by a freak wave in the Irish Sea.
4th February 2008

Following spread
Rosie Hallam
The Woolworths at the Angel, in Islington, north London, was one of the first to close. 8th October 2008

Carl Court
Two pairs of children's slippers are the only items remaining on a section of shelving in the Woolworths store in Camden, London. 11th December 2008

Facundo Arrizabalaga
Thick snow falls over London around Westminster Bridge on the night of the heaviest snowfall for 30 years. The severe weather seriously disrupted travel in the capital as forecasters warned of more heavy snowfalls across the country. 1st February 2009

Dan Kitwood GETTY IMAGES
A member of Snaresbrook High Court smokes next to a no smoking sign. 16th May 2008

Following spread
First Prize: News Folio
Peter Macdiarmid GETTY IMAGES
A broker on ICAP's dealing floor in London calls for prices as the markets react to the day's interest rate cut. 9th October 2008

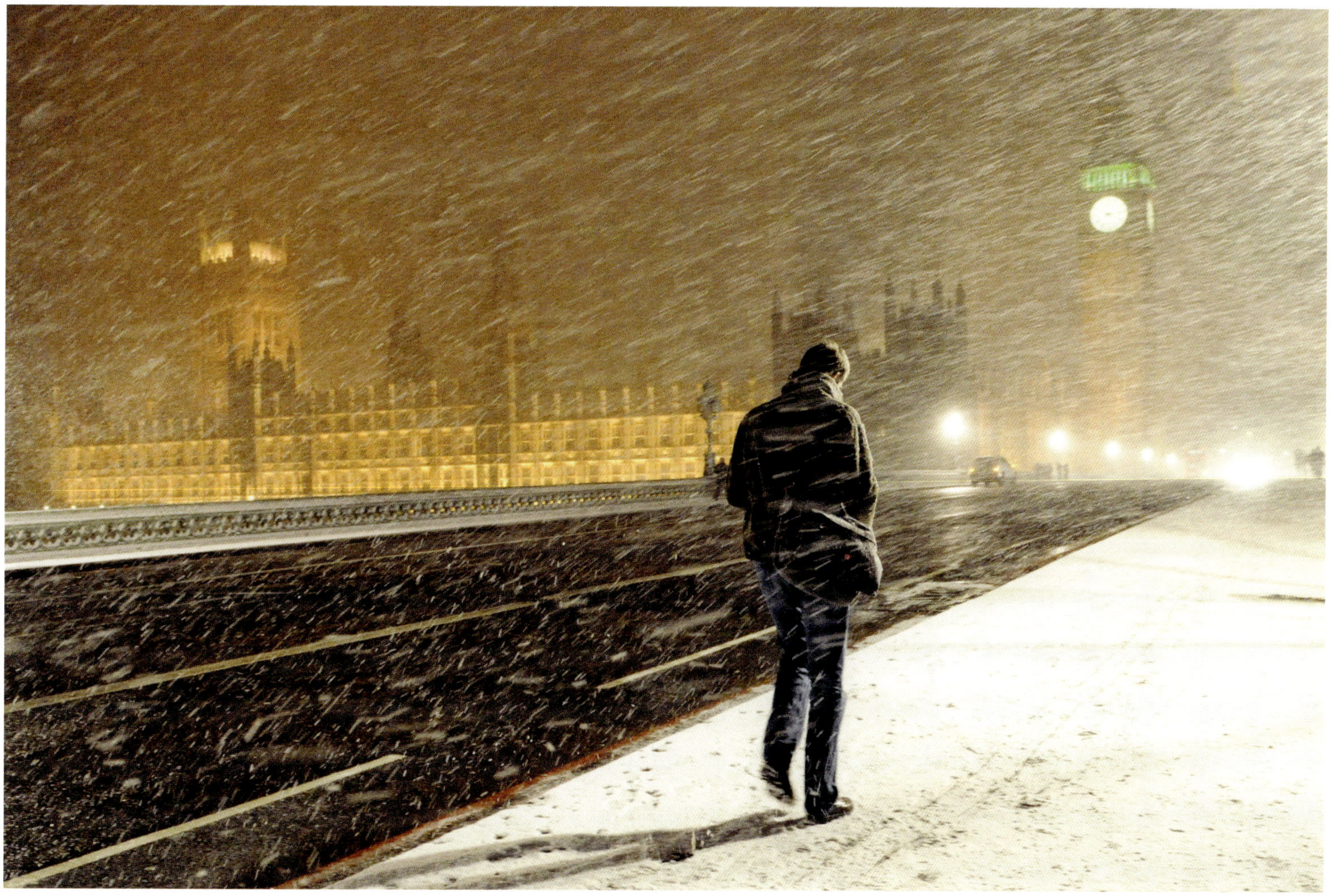

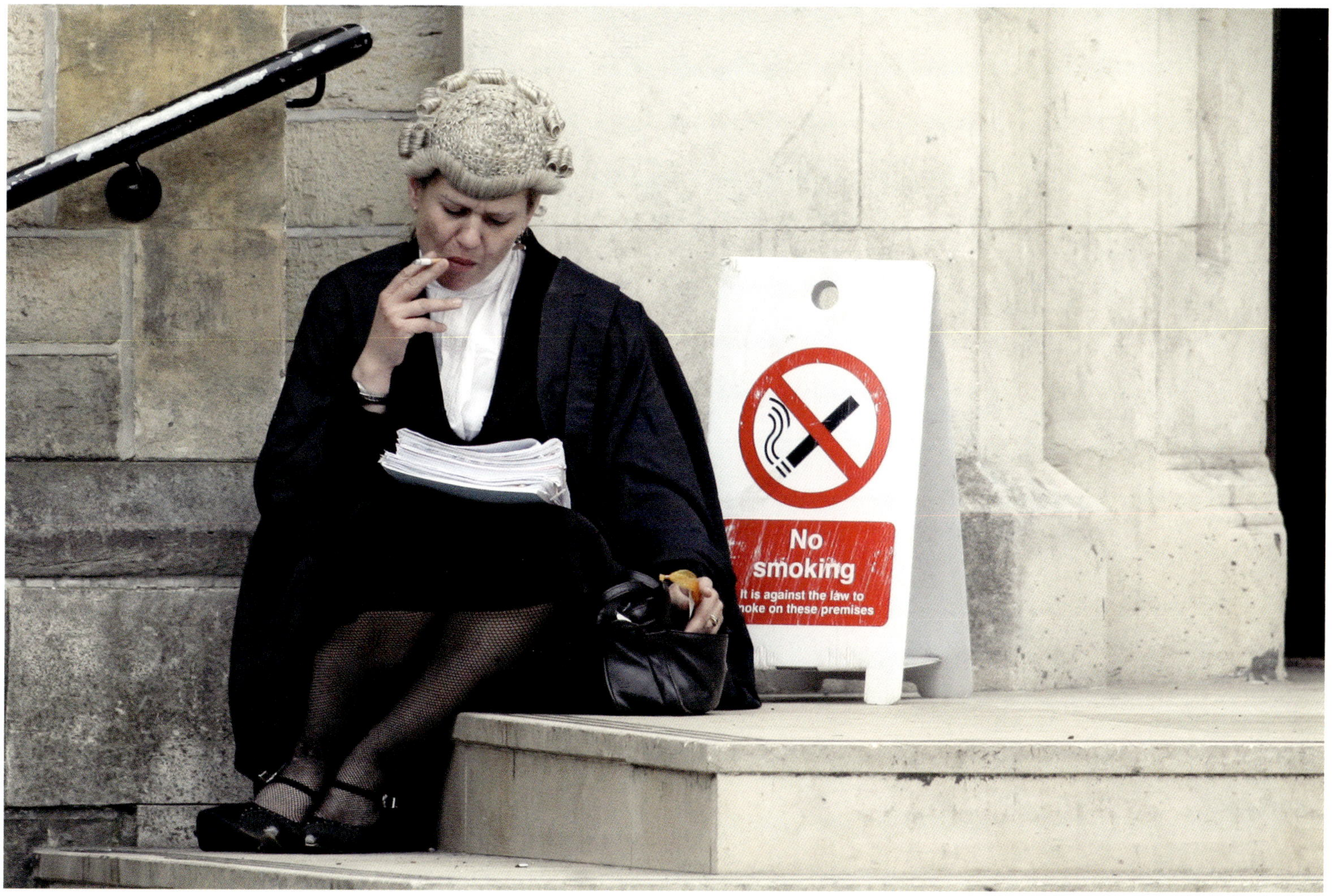
No
smoking
It is against the law to
oke on these premises

Eamon Ward THE CLARE PEOPLE
Jim Cronin with his four-year-old Percheron work horses at home in Ballyknavin, Co. Clare, Ireland. 22nd July 2008

Eamon Ward THE CLARE PEOPLE
George O'Halloran picking out stones from his garden at Ennistymon, Co Clare, Ireland. 29th April 2008

Graham Trott
Frank Naish and Paul Chant, Somerset cidermakers, at work on Frank's farm near Glastonbury. Frank is now 85 years old, but with help from Paul he keeps busy on the farm, looking after his orchards, hedge-laying, and making cider in the Autumn. Frank has lived on the family farm all his life, working alongside his older brother, Harold, who died in 2005. 4th December 2008

Eamon Ward

My Uncle Des lived all his life in the family home in Ennis, Co Clare, Ireland. I photographed the house and his possesions a week after he died, just as he had left them. 16th December 2008

Martin Godwin

Eddie O'Mahony, aged 88. In 1946, back from the war, Eddie and his young family moved into one of the prefab bungalows built as a temporary measure to combat Britain's housing shortage, due to bomb damage. The house was designed not to last more than a decade, but 62 years later Eddie is still there. Leaving the compact 55 sq m house he says, never entered his head; 'I wouldn't swap it for Buckingham Palace. Even if they included the Queen'. Catford, south London. 10th September 2008

Martin Godwin

Eddie O'Mahony. As previous. 10th September 2008

Adrian Dennis AGENCE FRANCE PRESSE

Demonstrators prepare to set off on the 'World Naked Bike Ride' in Hyde Park in London. Hundreds of naked participants protested against the destructive effects of car culture, for safer streets for pedestrians and cyclists, a stop to non-essential car use and more cycle lanes in British cities. 14th June 2008

Vicki Couchman

Maureen Wilson from Chorlton, Manchester, having a routine breast imaging mammogram, which she is called to have every two years after reaching the age of 50. She is with radiographer Lynn Lyle at the Kath Lock Mobile breast screening unit, part of the Knightingale Center at Wythenshawe Hospital, Manchester. 29th May 2008

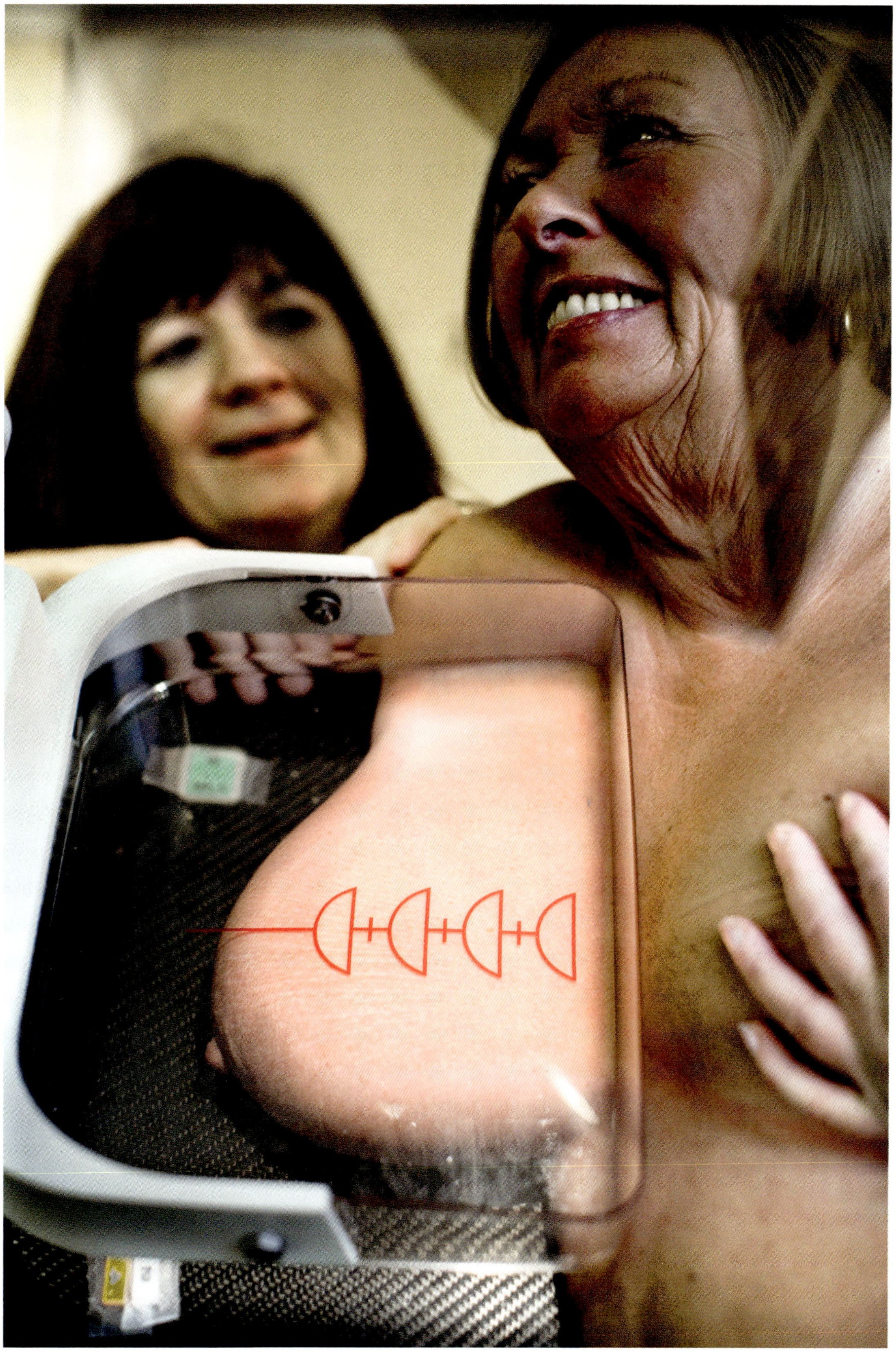

Jess Hurd REPORTDIGITAL.CO.UK
Bridesmaids get ready for the wedding of Irish travellers Nora Quilligan and Danny Sheridan from Dale Farm as they celebrate their wedding day. Many weddings are taking place ahead of the eviction of the travellers from their site near Basildon in Essex. 10th December 2008

CJ Clarke
Belfast, Northern Ireland 2008 Martina (far right) her friends and her little sister at home. Taken from the project 'Forgotten Union – Belfast Now' which documents the lives, habits and environment of the Protestant community in contemporary Belfast, with a particular focus on youth culture. 11th November 2008

Matt Kirwan SWNS
Jacob Lamb received a faulty Superman suit as a gift. When his mother Debbie rang up Marks & Spencers to organise a refund, the sales assistant would only speak to Jacob aged 7. 4th September 2008

Bruno Vincent
A wingsuit flyer passes over the Aguille Du Midi after jumping from a helicopter above Mont Blanc during the Nissan Outdoor Games in Chamonix, France. The riders reached lateral speeds of 140 kph before pulling their parachutes and landing in Chamonix town. 16th February 2008

Callum Bennetts MAVERICK
Circus OZ's iconic red kangaroos perform acrobatic feats on top of Edinburgh's Carlton Hill during the Edinburgh Festival Fringe. These urban bounding beasts take part in the show which features a spectacular team of acrobats, aerialists and musicians with some added cheeky Australian humour. 1st August 2008

Thomas Main
Eleven-year-old diver Grace Reid during a practice session at the Royal Commonwealth Pool in Edinburgh, Scotland. 5th March 2008

Jane Barlow
Gannets at the start of the breeding season on Bass
Rock off the East Lothian coast in Scotland, the largest
single island gannet colony in the world. 15th April 2008

Dan Chung THE GUARDIAN
Boys play in the swamp in the Ugandan village of Katine.
The village has benefited from an aid programme run
by the NGO AMREF working in association with the
Guardian newspaper. 15th December 2008

Following spread

Christopher Furlong GETTY IMAGES
A seagull flies past a viewing telescope in Rhyl, Wales. Rhyl was once an elegant Victorian seaside destination on the North Wales coast and one of Britain's premier seaside resorts, but with the advent of cheap flights abroad and guaranteed sunshine the holiday resort has suffered. The town was recently put in the top 10% most deprived areas of Wales and has been the centre of a regeneration project, including the £85 million Ocean Plaza complex on the site of the former Ocean Beach Fun Fair. 6th October 2008

Toby Madden
Weligama is a small village on the southern coast of Sri Lanka between Galle and Matara where the Stilt Fishermen can be found. It is a strange technique of fishing and nobody knows how or where this technique originated. They make their own stilts on the reef and all stilts are owned by individual fisher families. They collect their day's catch in the basket and carry it ashore. Stilt-fishing is a seasonal profession as during the south-western monsoon the seas become too rough to stay comfortably perched on a stick, 30 yards offshore. During November, and through to around the end of March, these fisherman are a common sight along the southern coast of Sri Lanka. 1st January 2008

Sam Furlong SWNS
A Belgian F-16 jet fighter practises manoeuvres at RAF Fairford in Gloucestershire before the event was cancelled due to heavy rain. 11th July 2008

Peter Macdiarmid GETTY IMAGES
Swimmers take an early morning dip in the Hampton heated outdoor pool near London. Regular swimmers use the pool, which is heated to 28 degrees centigrade, 365 days a year. This particular morning the air temperature was only 1° C above freezing. At one time London could boast more that 50 open-air pools – currently there are about 15 operating in and around the capital. 10th December 2008

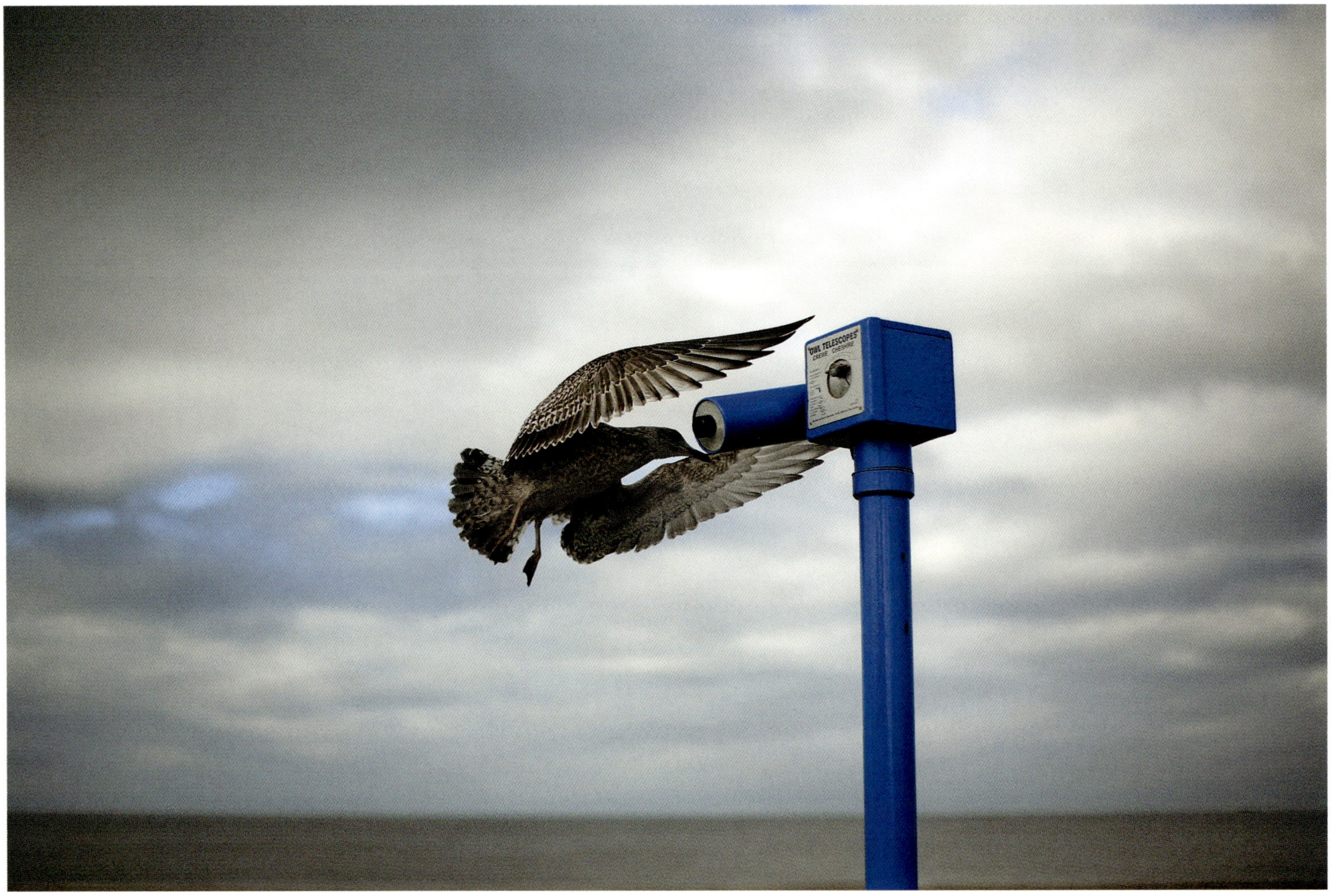
'OWL TELESCOPES'
CREWE CHESHIRE

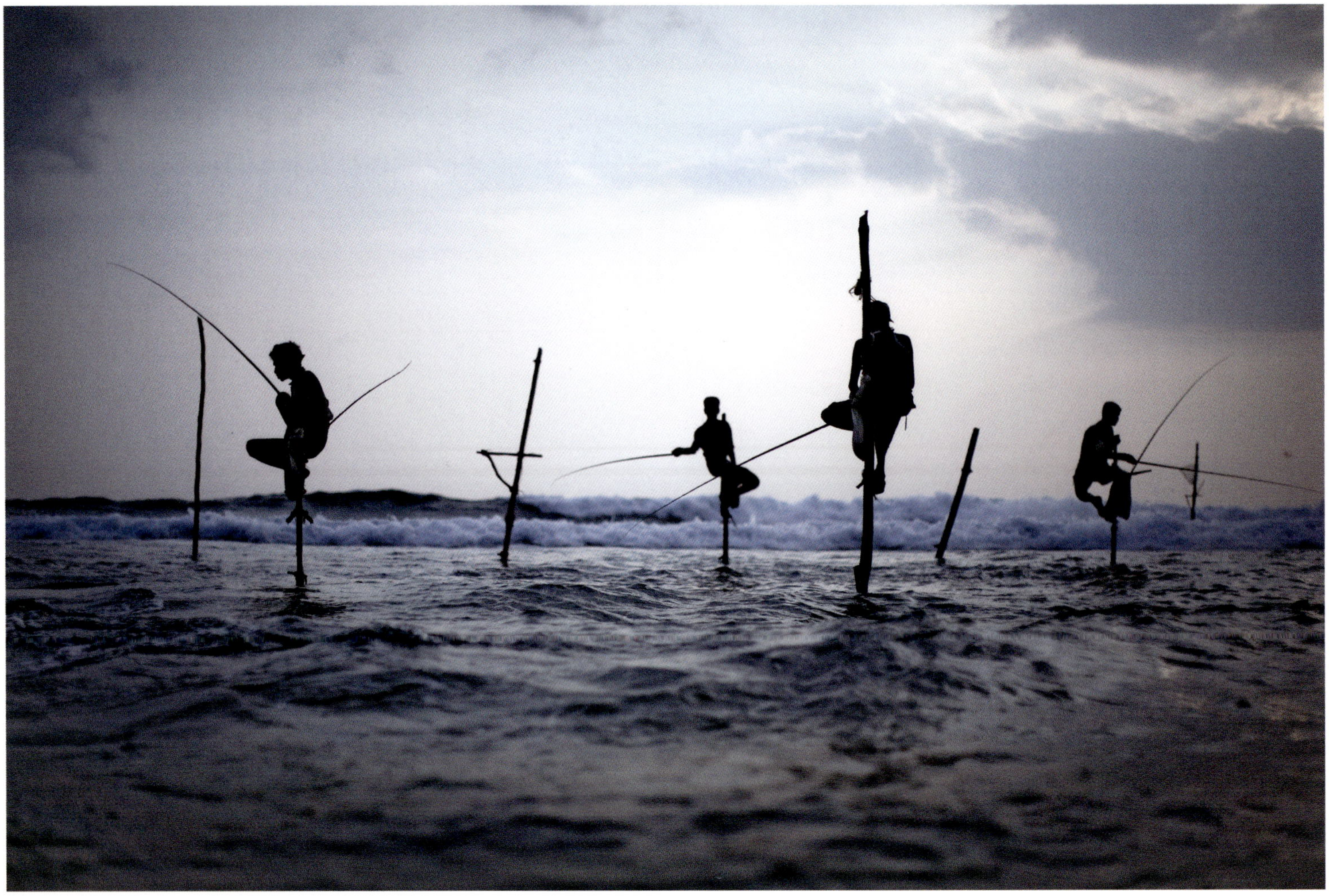

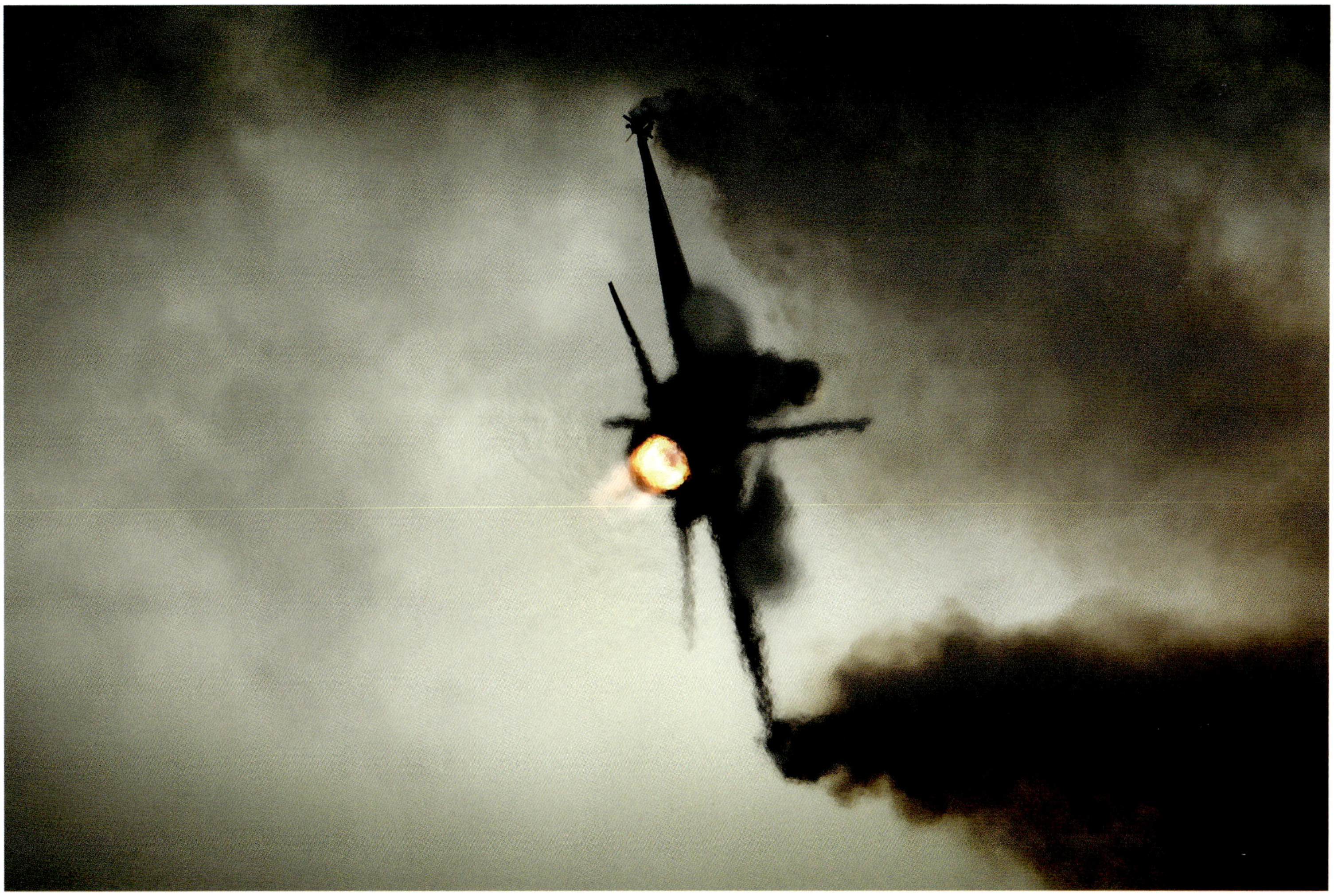

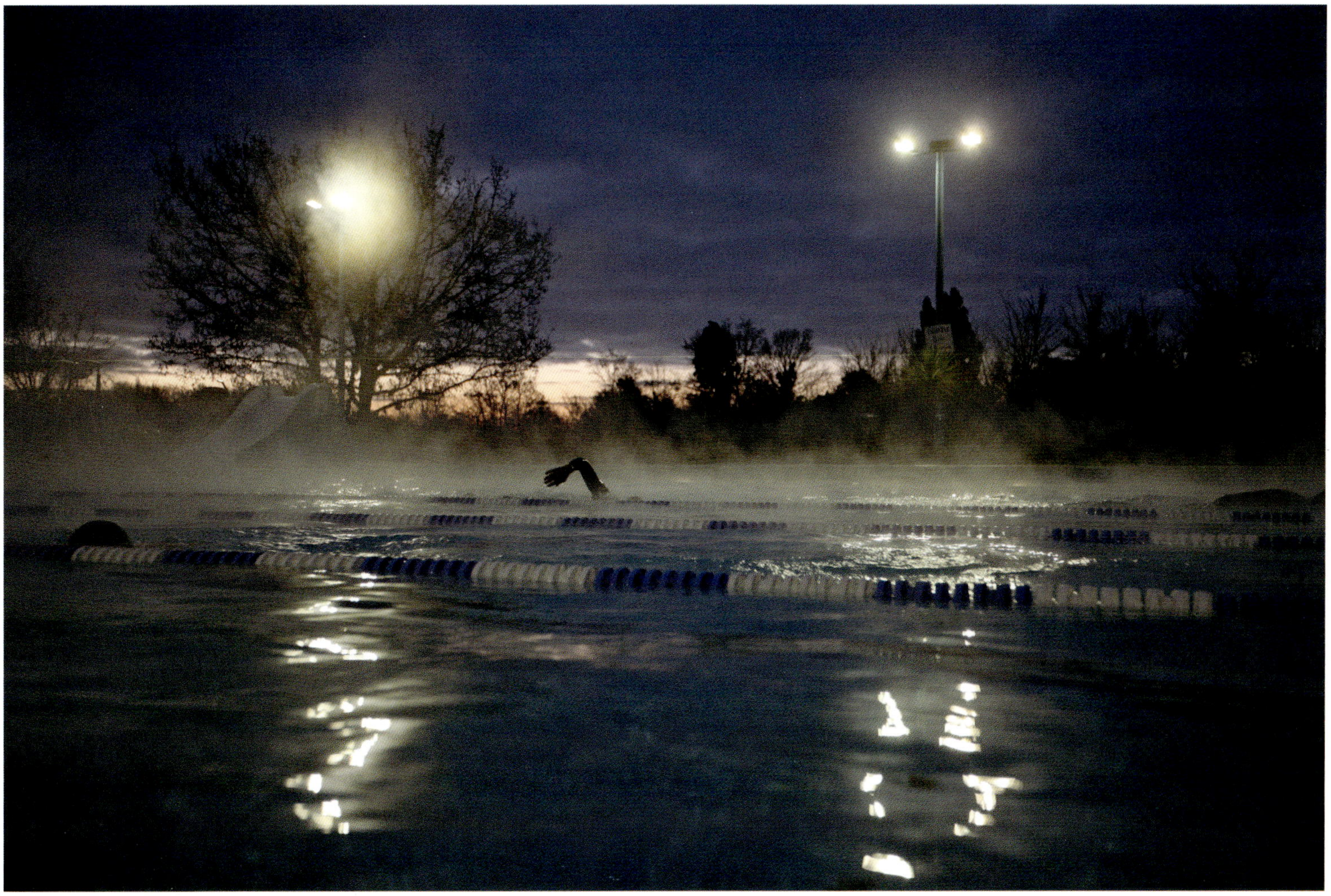

Anthony Devlin PRESS ASSOCIATION
Around 250,000 plastic ducks destined for the Great
British Duck Race on a 1km stretch of the River Thames
near Hampton Court Palace, London. Now in its second
year, the race raises money for charities including
Downs Syndrome Association, WaterAid and the
NSPCC. It cost £2 to enter a duck and the winner
received a £10,000 prize. 31st August 2008

Rui Vieira PRESS ASSOCIATION
A 44-year-old gorilla called Joe, eating a pear on the day
Twycross Zoo celebrated its 45th birthday. 19th May 2008

Graeme Robertson

A UK animal testing laboratory that could not be identified for security reasons. 15th May 2008

Christopher Pledger

Judging takes place at the 2008 World Budgerigar Championship Show in Doncaster, England.

27th September 2008

Irina Kalashnikova
North Koreans perform at the Arirang Festival at the May Day stadium in Pyongyang. The biggest and the best of the annual mass games festivals where up to 100,000 dancers and gymnasts perform to tell the story of the formation of the Democratic People's Republic of Korea. 4th August 2008

Irina Kalashnikova
Public beach in Wonsan city, 200 km away from Pyongyang. There are many beaches on the coastline of East Sea of Korea. The Songdowan foreign visitors beach is mainly occupied by North Koreans who can afford to pay the entrance fee, rather than utilize the crowded public beach next door. 7th August 2008

Irina Kalashnikova
Children at the Kim Jong Suk Nursery would normally sit around a model of the Mangyongdae birthplace of Kim Il Sung and chant revolutionary nursery rhymes. The first year of education is largely based around learning of the birthplace and early history of Kim Il Sung, while the second focuses on the guerrilla struggles around Mount Paekdu and the secret revolutionary camp. Pyongyang, North Korea. 11th August 2008

Following spread
First Prize: News
David Bebber
Ken Livingstone visits Ken's Cafe on Green Street, east
London, after unveiling a new campaign poster at the
West Ham football ground during London's Mayoral
elections. 30th April 2008

Following spread
First Prize: Portraits
Leon Neal AGENCE FRANCE PRESSE
The Ukrainian President Viktor Yushchenko speaks
to the media outside No 10 Downing Street in London
Following a meeting with British Prime Minster
Gordon Brown. 15th January 2009

Dominic Lipinski PRESS ASSOCIATION
Dame Vera Lynn, aged 92, attends the launch of the
new 'The Times of my Life' website, at the Cabinet War
Rooms, Westminster, central London. 30th September 2008

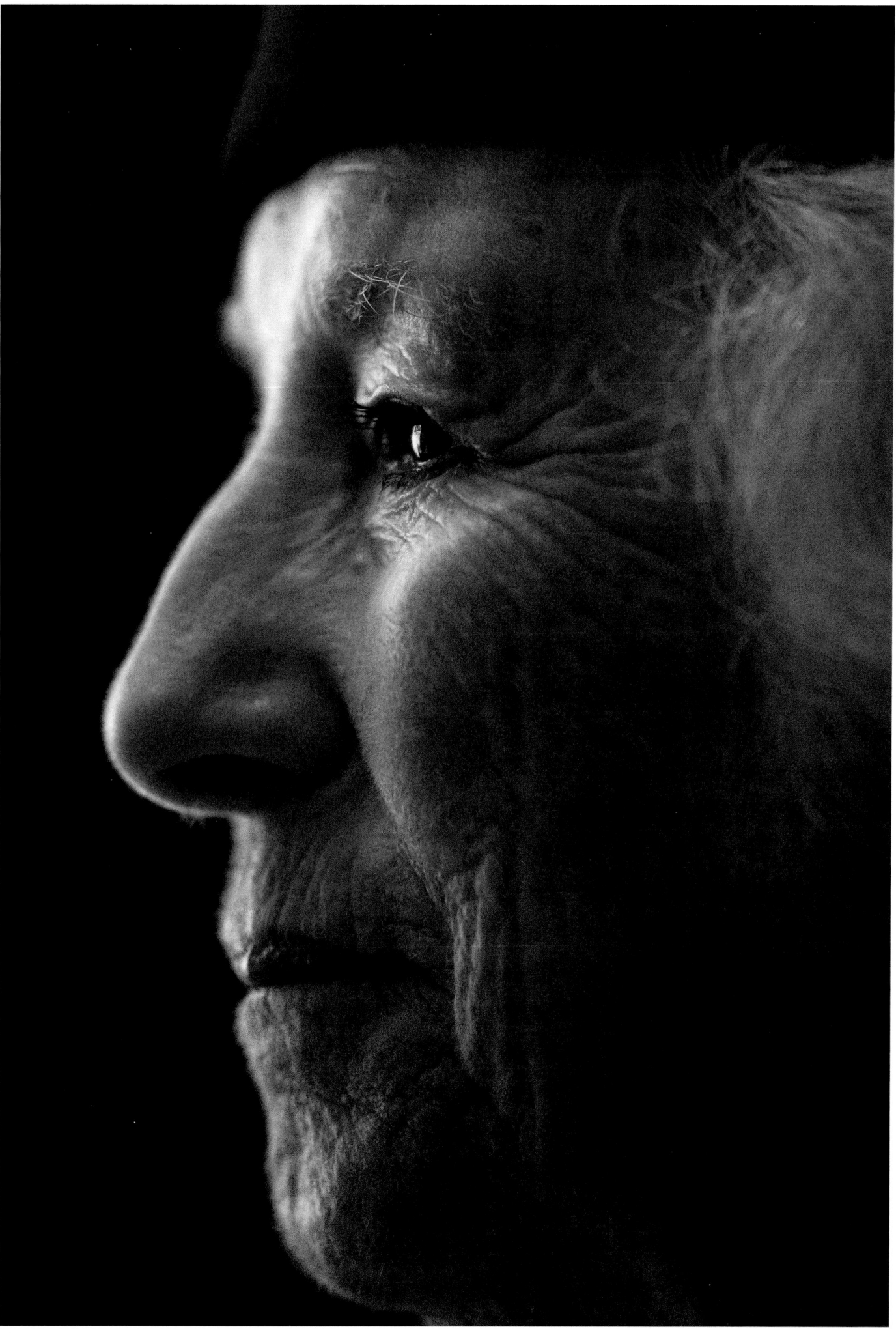

Tom Pilston
Bathed in the light of giant TV screens, Americans listen to Barack Obama, America's first African American President, give his victory speech in Grant Park, Chicago.
4th November 2008

Edmond Terakopian
US Democratic presidential candidate Barack Obama visits British Prime Minister Gordon Brown at No 10 Downing Street in London. Senator Obama was on the final part of the European leg of his world tour.
26th July 2008

Bruce Adams DAILY MAIL
Gordon Brown shakes the hand of his Foreign Secretary David Mlliband after his speech at the Labour Party conference at the G-Mex centre in Manchester.
22nd September 2008

First Prize: News Folio
Peter Macdiarmid GETTY IMAGES
Prime Minister Gordon Brown looks down as he waits to meet European Commission President José Manuel Barroso in Downing Street. 5th June 2008

Following spread
Tom Pilston
The comedian Russell Brand, photographed in London. 8th October 2008

Graeme Robertson
The British fashion designer Vivienne Westwood. 14th November 2008

Shaun Curry AGENCE FRANCE PRESSE
Heather Mills addresses the media outside London's High Court as she and her estranged husband, pop legend Paul McCartney, agreed a divorce deal worth nearly £25 million. 17th March 2008

Lee Thompson CHRISTIAN AID
John Odima, a witch doctor in Barak Obama's ancestral home of Kogelo in Kenya. The 91-year-old claimed that he helped Mr. Obama become President of the USA. 17th December 2008

Following spread
Graham Trott
One of a series of portraits taken at a London based Asset Management company. 30th April 2008

Daniel Lynch
Tim Marlow, Director of Exhibitions for the White Cube gallery, photographed at the White Cube in St. James's, London. 5th March 2008

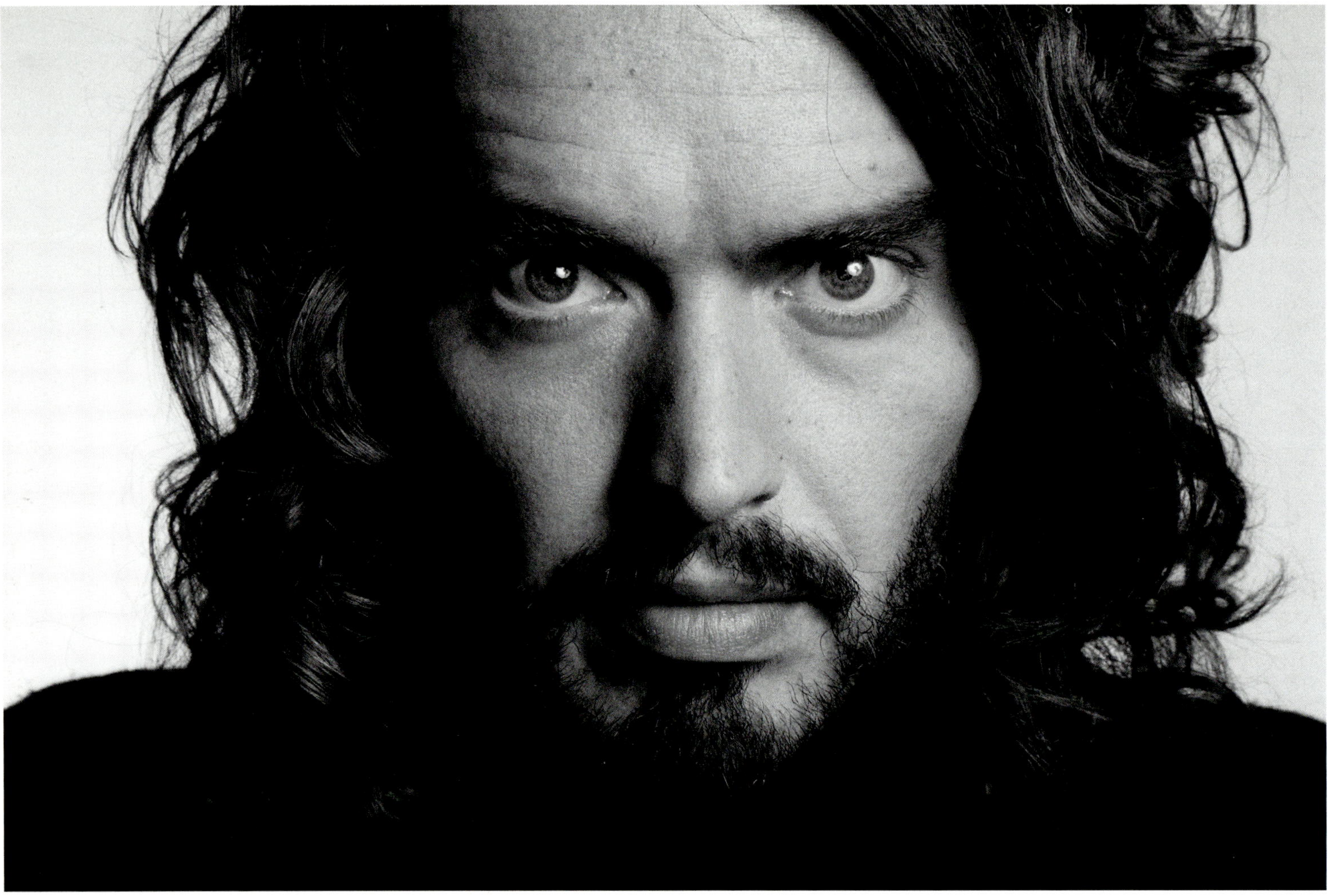

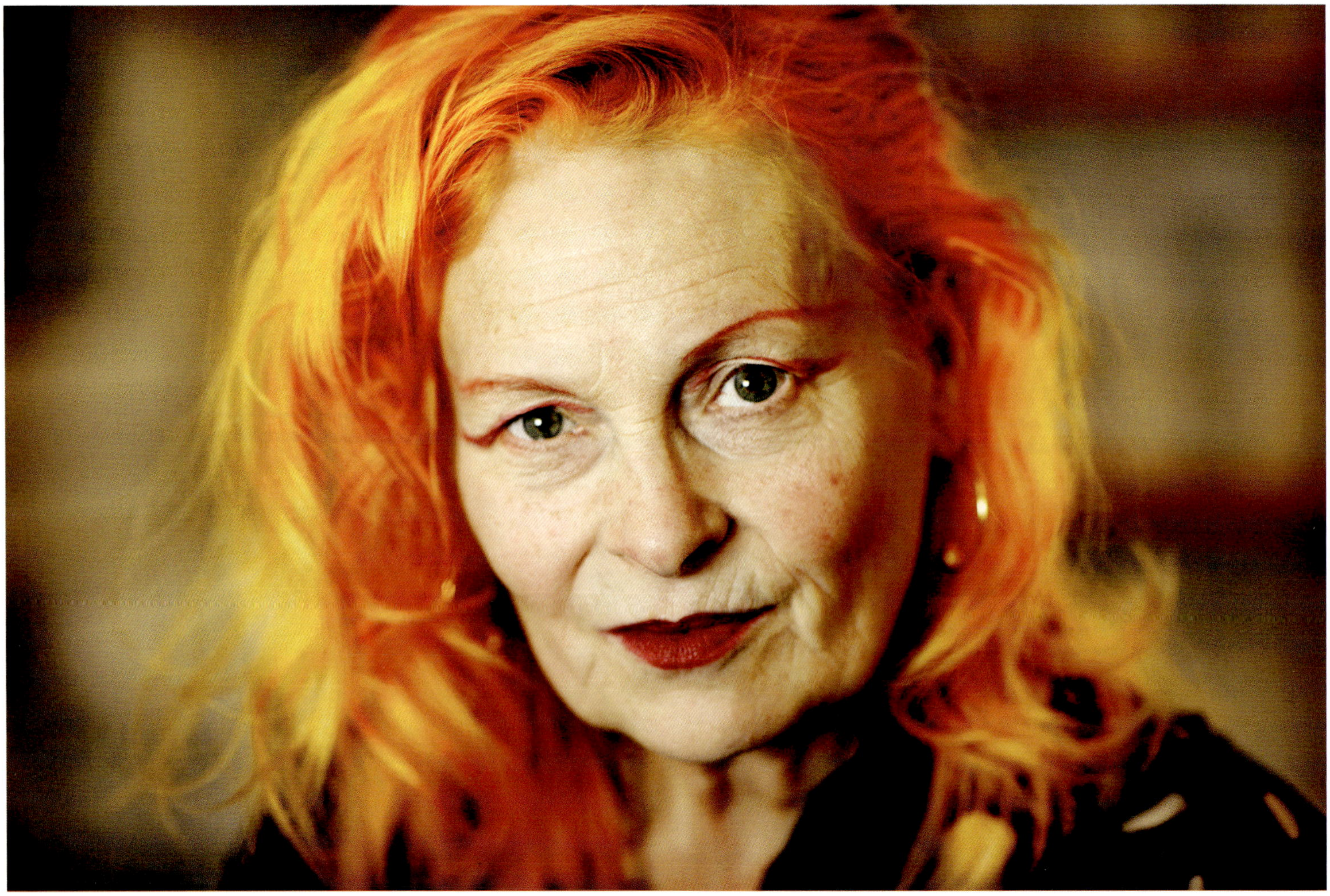

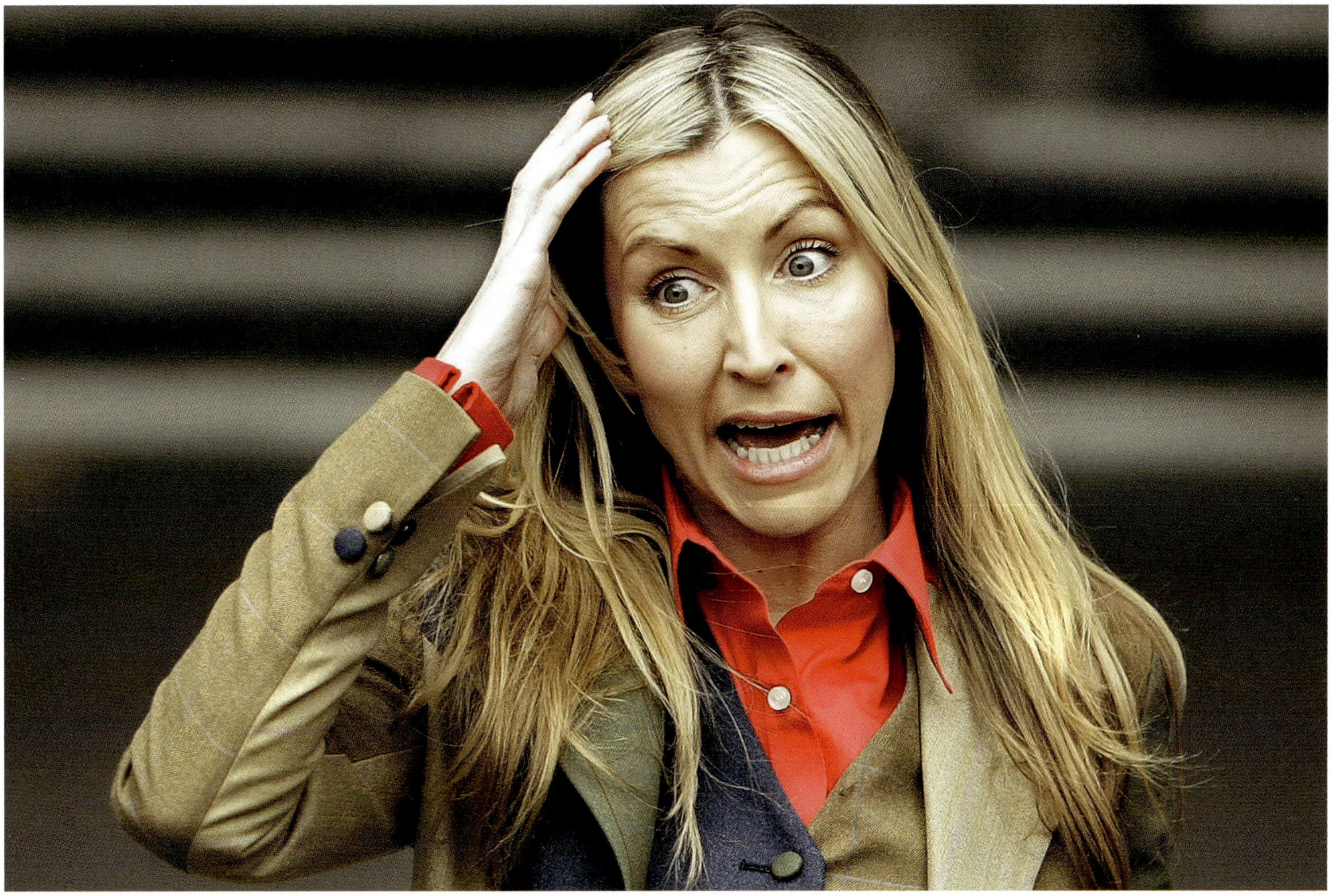
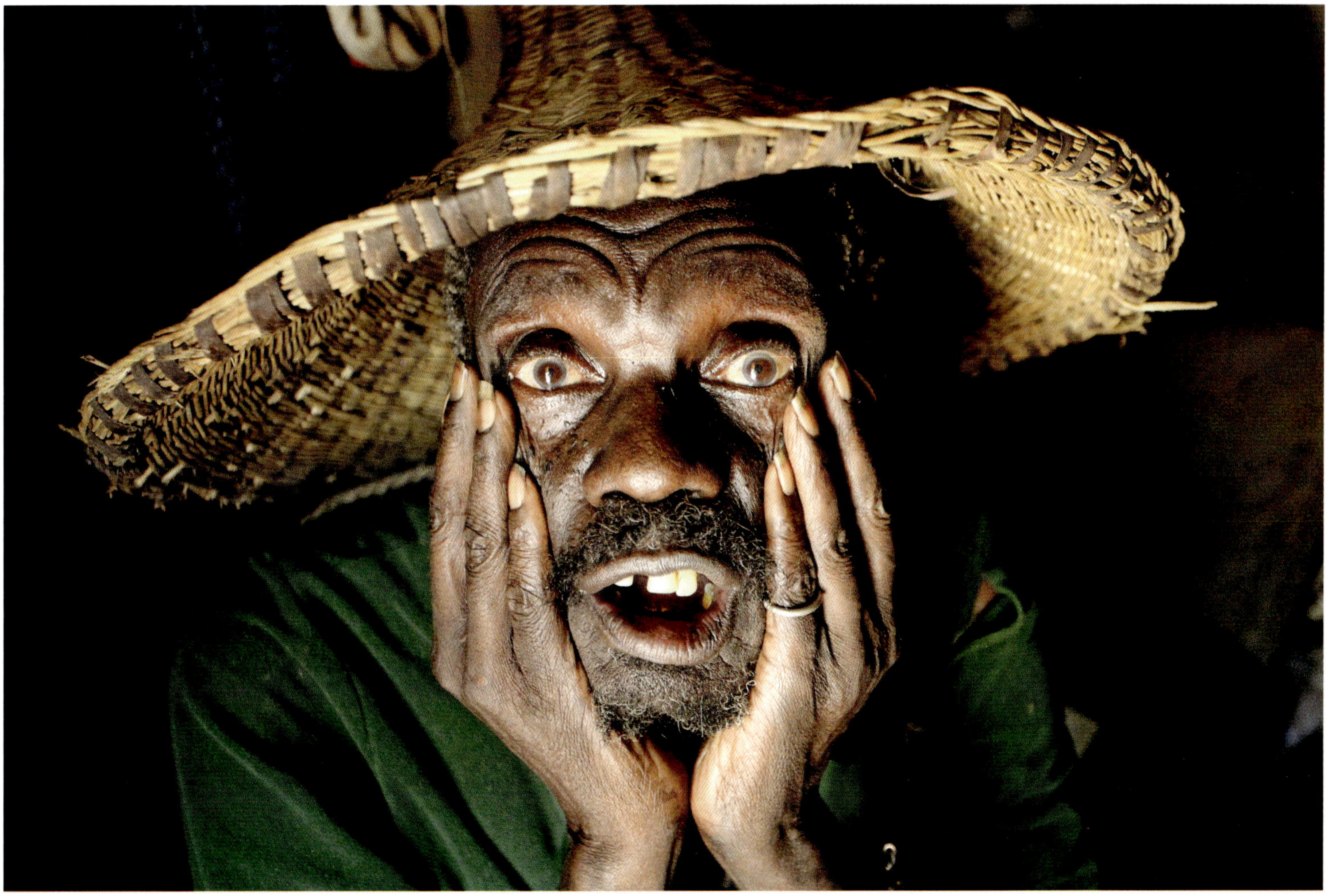

Warren Little GETTY IMAGES
Celebrity chef Gordon Ramsay accepts water from a
photographer after crossing the finishing line in the
2008 Flora London Marathon. 13th April 2008

Lefteris Pitarakis ASSOCIATED PRESS
Deep under a pine-tree-covered mountain, men
clamber into red overalls and heavy boots, strap on
lamps and attach sensors that monitor gas levels,
at a coal mine near Cwmgrach, Wales. 27th August 2008

Julien Behal PRESS ASSOCIATION
James 'Indian' McCook pictured in his pigeon loft in his
back yard outside the village of Armoy, North Antrim
in Northern Ireland. The legendary hard man worked
as a bouncer and door man for years and his toughness
meant that he was sought out over the years by
potential challengers for bare knuckle bouts. Born in
1928, he is 'king' of the North Antrim hardmen. It's a
title he would make no comment on, perhaps indicating
nothing more than a shrug of the shoulders or a smile,
but which would attract nods of approval from those
who have heard about his awesome reputation.
5th February 2008

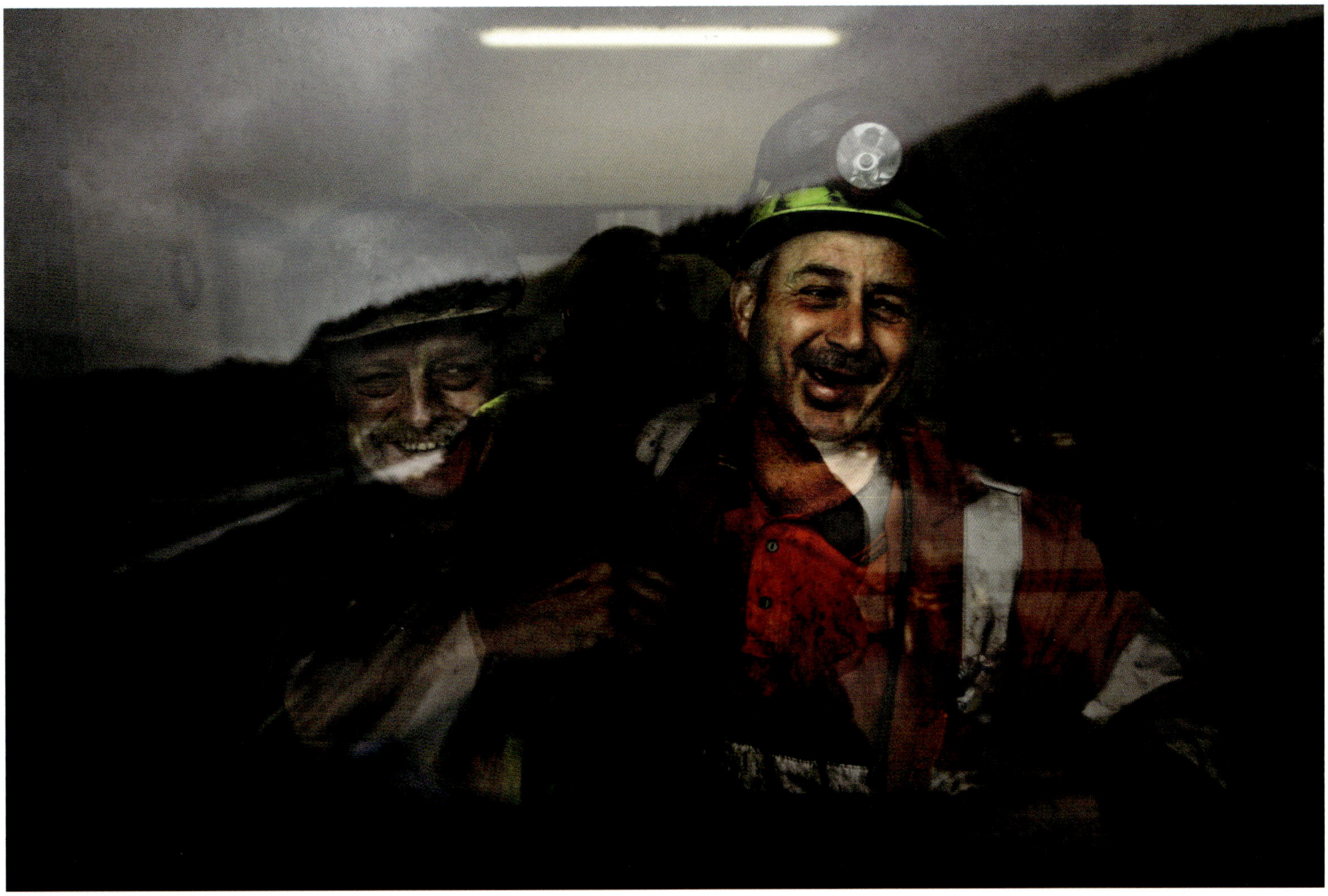

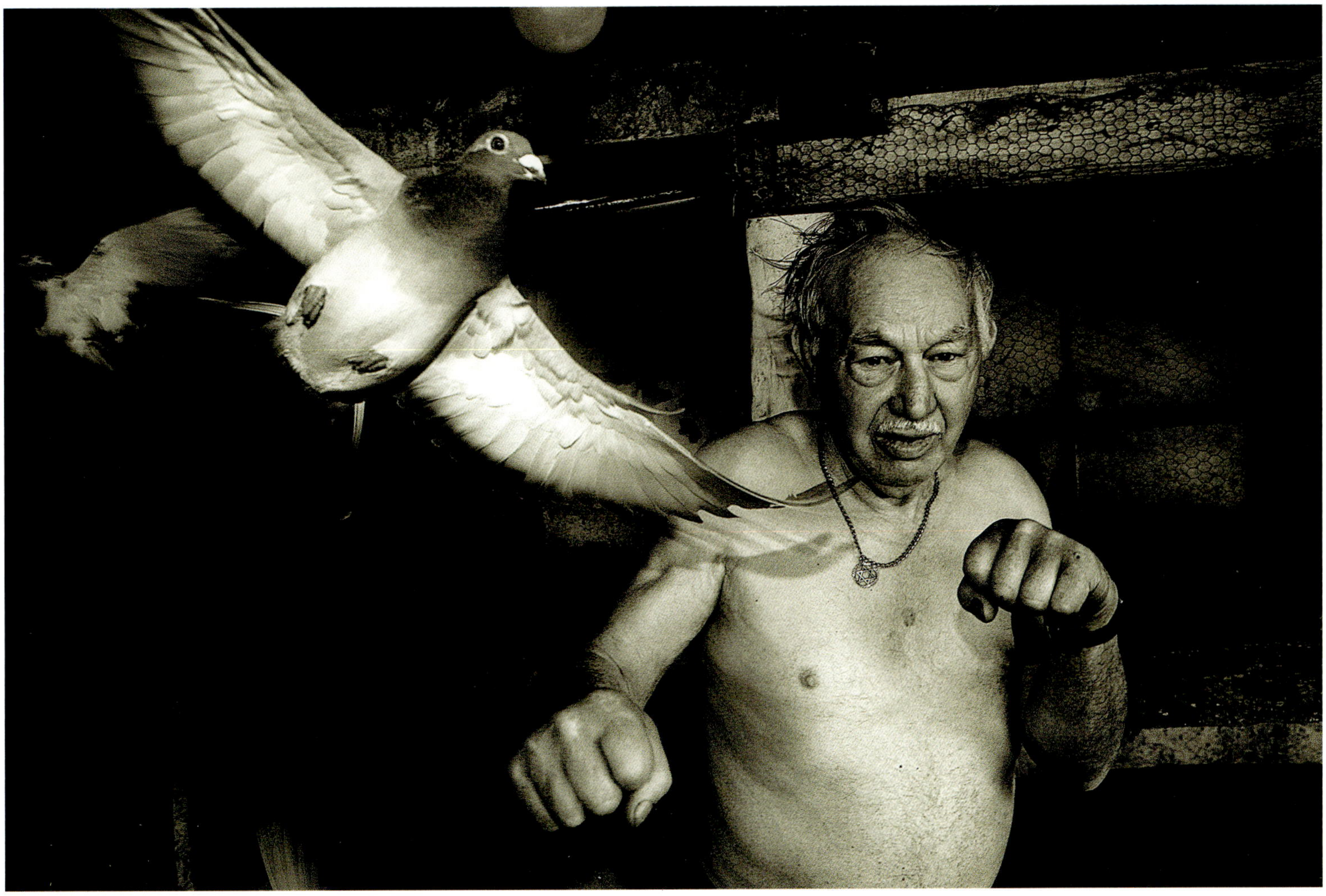

First Prize: News Folio
Peter Macdiarmid GETTY IMAGES

British singer Amy Winehouse sits on stage and looks up at a television monitor whilst awaiting news of a possible Grammy Award at The Riverside Studios in London. The singer went on to dominate the 50th Grammy Awards, winning five that night.
10th February 2008

James Horan PHOTOCALL IRELAND

Michael Sheehan, from Galway, winner of the heavyweight 90kg+ category, pictured getting his fake tan applied before going on stage at the Republic of Ireland Body Building Federation National Championships, held at the Millennium Theatre in Limerick. 4th October 2008

Eddie Mulholland THE DAILY TELEGRAPH

The actress Wendy Richard married her partner John Burns in a civil ceremony in London shortly after revealing that she would start chemotherapy again, having battled breast cancer twice before. She died in February 2009. 10th October 2008

Following spread

Christopher Furlong GETTY IMAGES
A figure from Antony Gormley's 'Another Place' welcomes one of the Tall Ships to Merseyside as it sails past the Burbo Bank wind farm on the approach to the Port of Liverpool. As the European City of Culture, Liverpool hosted part of the Tall Ships racing festival. Up to one hundred of these sailing ships went on display to the public, and event organisers expected crowds of up to one million people before their race to Norway began. 18th July 2008

David Levene
'normally, proceeding and unrestricted with without title, 2008' by Gelitin. An artwork on a roof terrace at the Hayward Gallery, which is a boating lake complete with a dock and three small wooden boats. Part of the Psycho Buildings show on London's South Bank. 26th May 2008

Laurence Griffiths
A family cricket match on South Sands Beach, Devon. 8th August 2008

David Bebber
A wedding party drives through Cuba's capital Havana in one of the city's famous classic cars. 21st February 2008

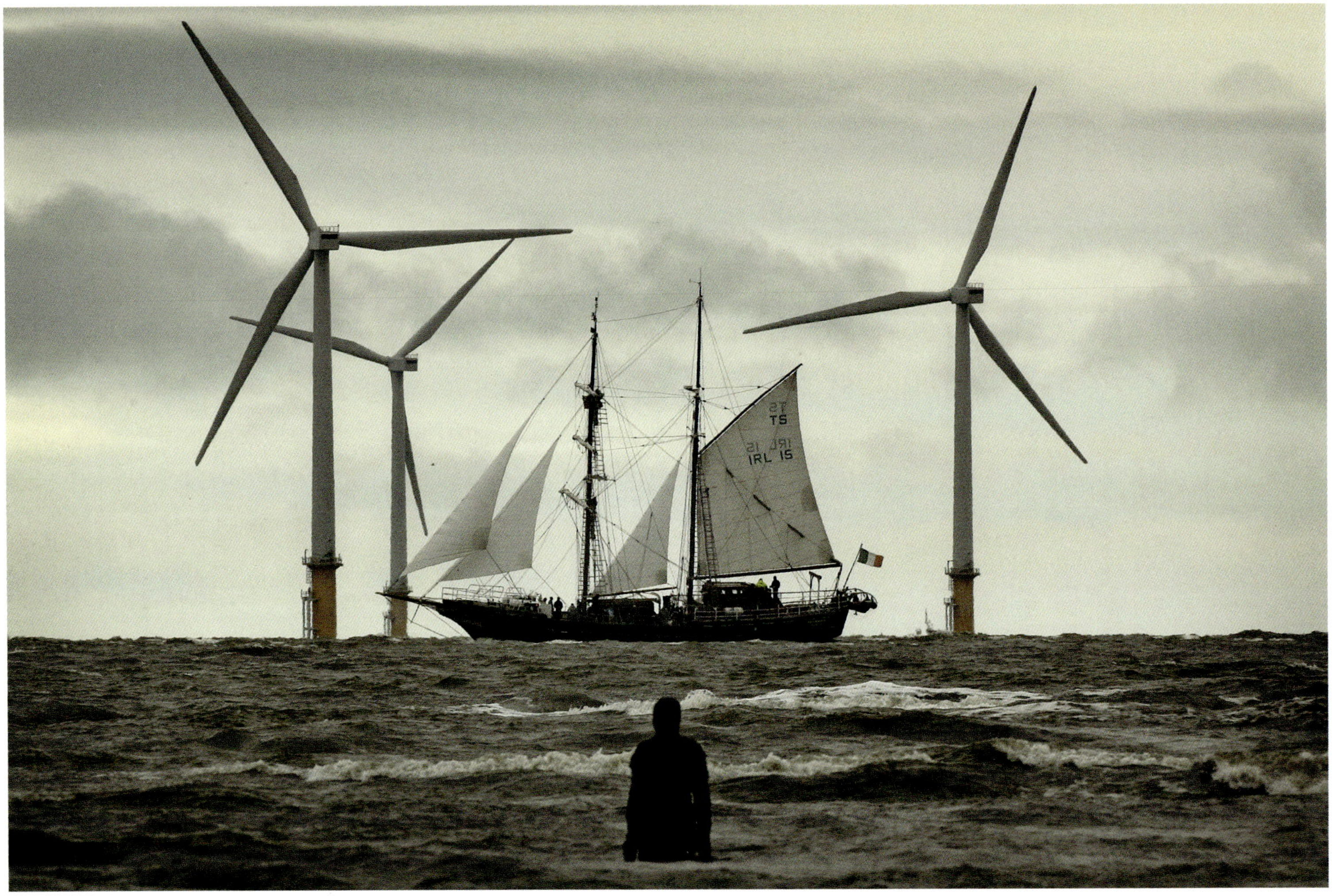
TS
IRL 15

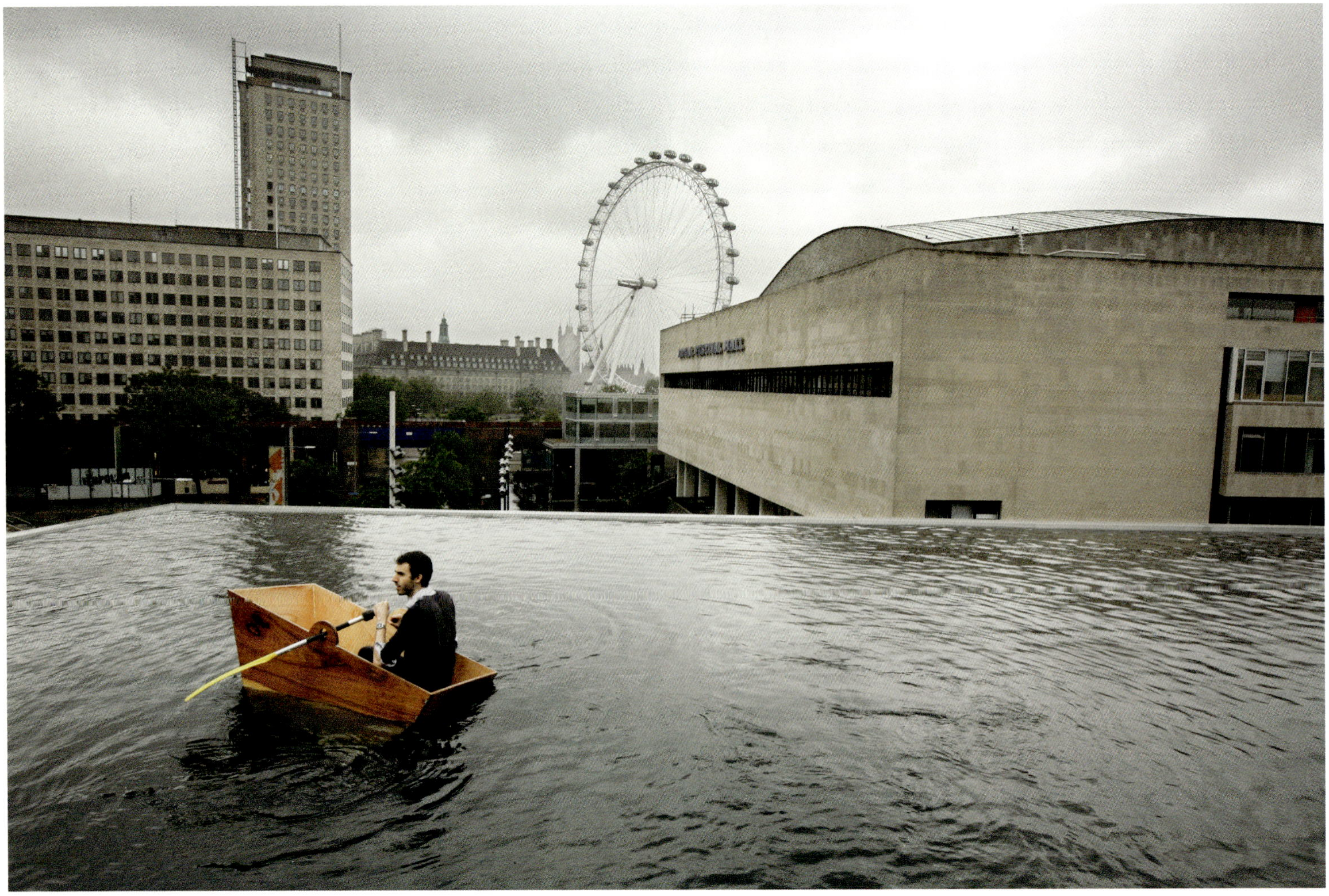

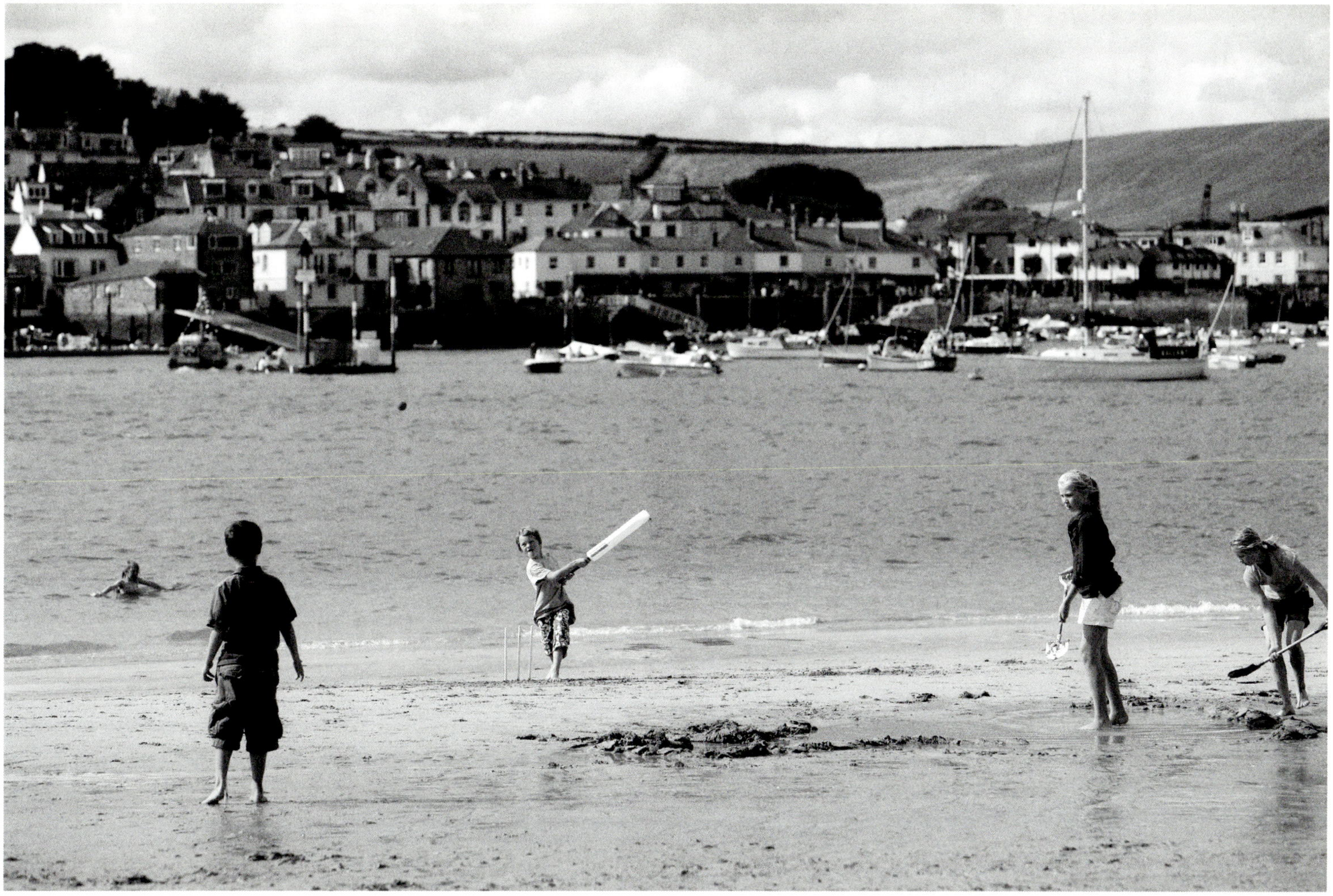

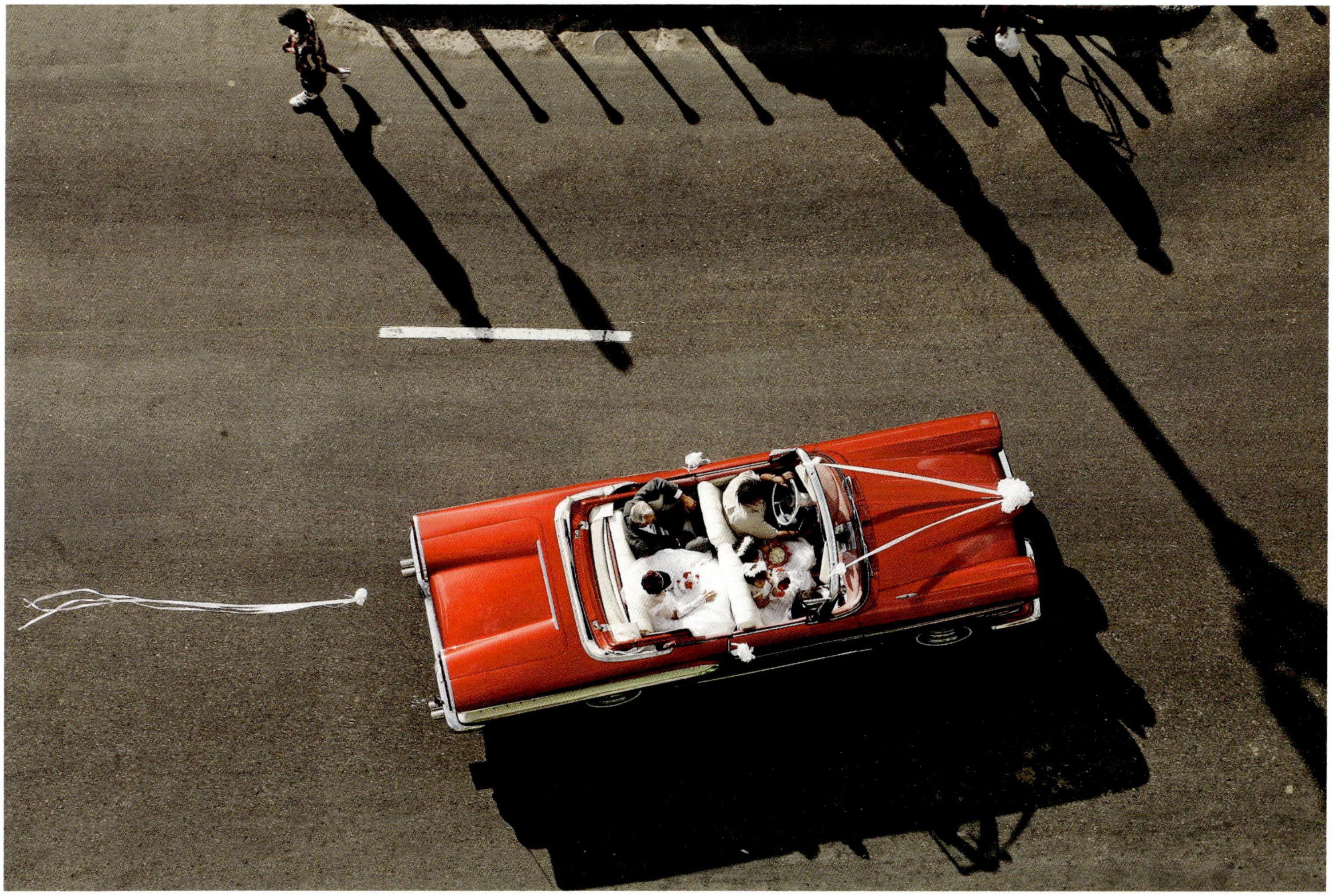

First Prize: The Arts

Mark Waugh MANCHESTER EVENING NEWS
The Royal Collection contains the world's most important group of drawings by Leonardo da Vinci. 'Skull section – 1489' was one of ten exhibited at Manchester Art Gallery as a celebration of Prince Charles' 60th birthday. 28th February 2008

Christopher Furlong GETTY IMAGES
The Duke and Duchess of Devonshire view a giant sculpture of a seven-month-old baby by artist Marc Quinn entitled 'Planet' in the gardens of their home, Chatsworth House near Bakewell in Derbyshire, England. The bronze sculpture painted white was part of the 'Beyond Limits' exhibition of modern and contemporary sculpture displayed in the gardens of Chatsworth by Sotheby's. In past years acclaimed artists Damien Hirst, Antony Gormley, Salvador Dali and Henry Moore have had work exhibited. 4th September 2008

David Bebber
Fancy dress in the cabaret field at the Glastonbury
festival, Somerset. 29th June 2008

David Bebber
A racegoer negotiates some steps as she arrives on
the first day of Royal Ascot, Berkshire. 17th June 2008

Roger Bamber
An old Brighton Pier 'Hall of Mirrors' distorting mirror
reflects four children on a family outing on Brighton
seafront. Jack Etherton (8), Susie Gilbert (10), Tim
Etherton (7) and Alisha Gilbert (8), give a big hand
to their bizarre reflections. 8th August 2008

Les Wilson
Elsa Amiss, aged eleven, with one of the ducks from her
parents' Higher Fingle Farm in Devon. 10th September 2008

Chris Jackson GETTY IMAGES
Camilla, Duchess of Cornwall tours the stables at the
Olympia Horse Show in London. The Duchess met
competitors and horses backstage at the event as
well as presenting awards. 17th December 2008

First Prize: Royalty & Entertainment
Mark Stewart
Zara Phillips faces disappointment after knocking
fences down whilst competing at the Festival of
Eventing at Gatcombe Park, then receives some
words of advice from her mother, the Princess Royal.
3rd August 2008

Bruce Adams DAILY MAIL
Two racegoers share a joke during Ladies' Day at the
Grand National Meeting at Aintree, near Liverpool.
4th April 2008

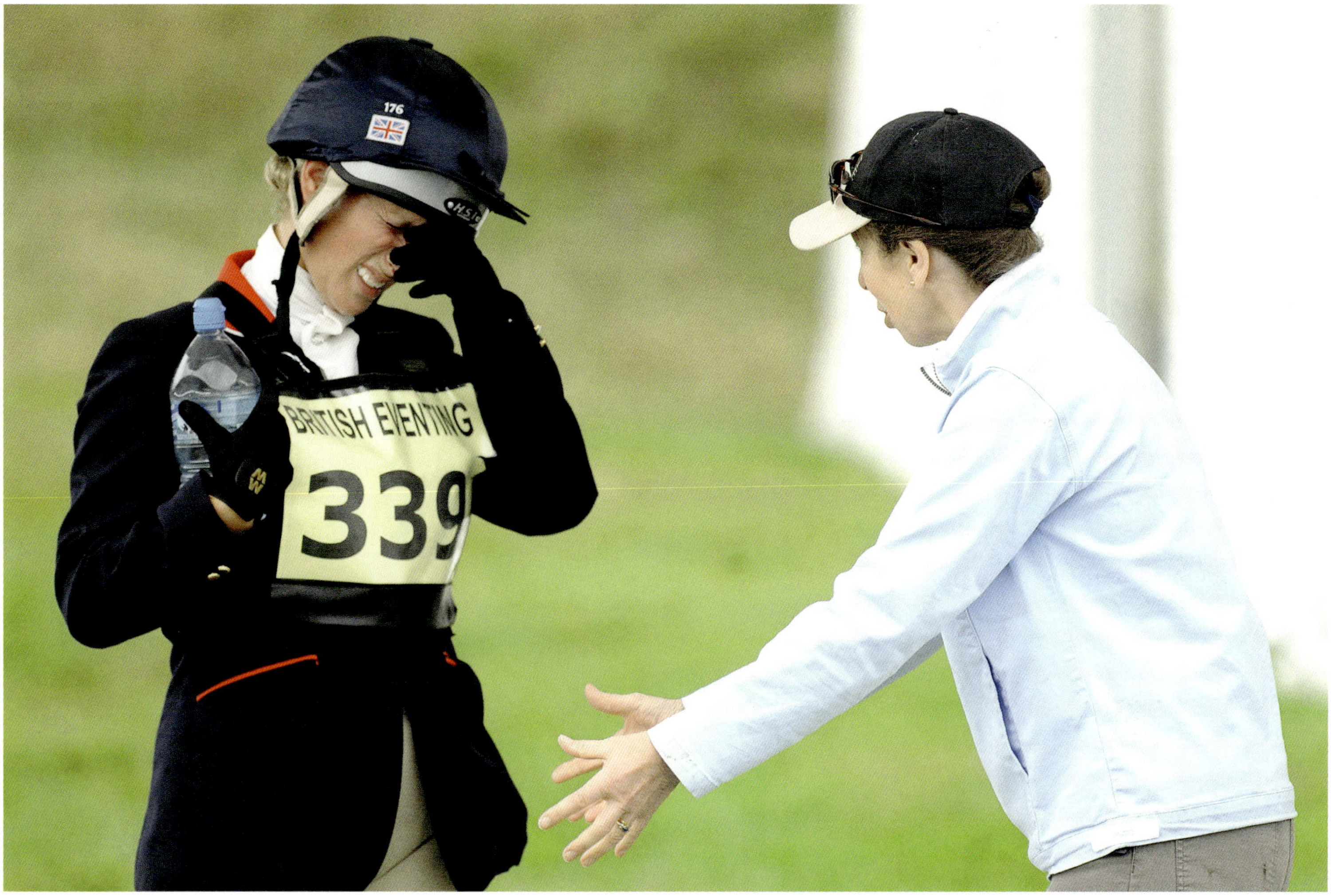
176
BRITISH EVENTING
339

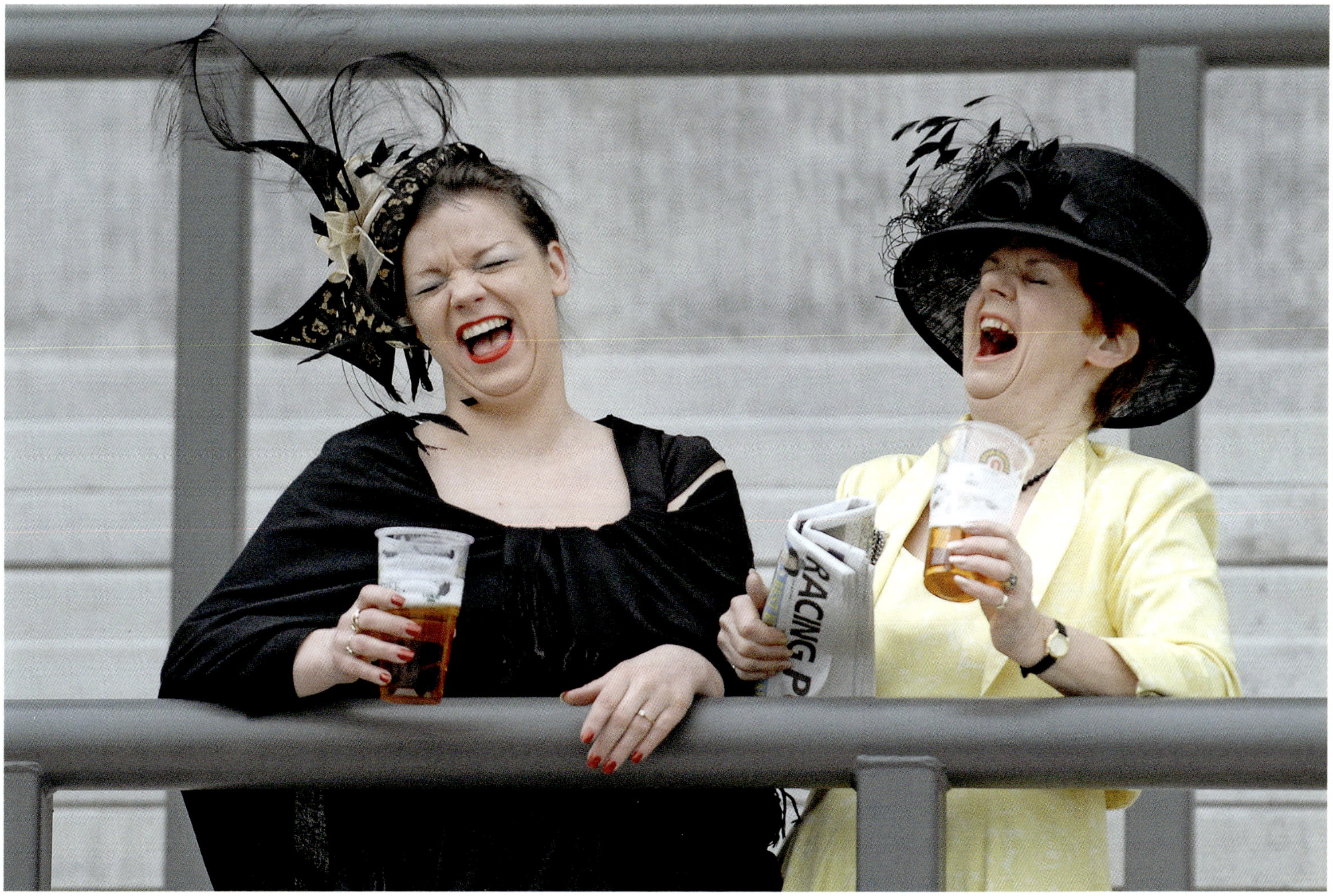
RACING P

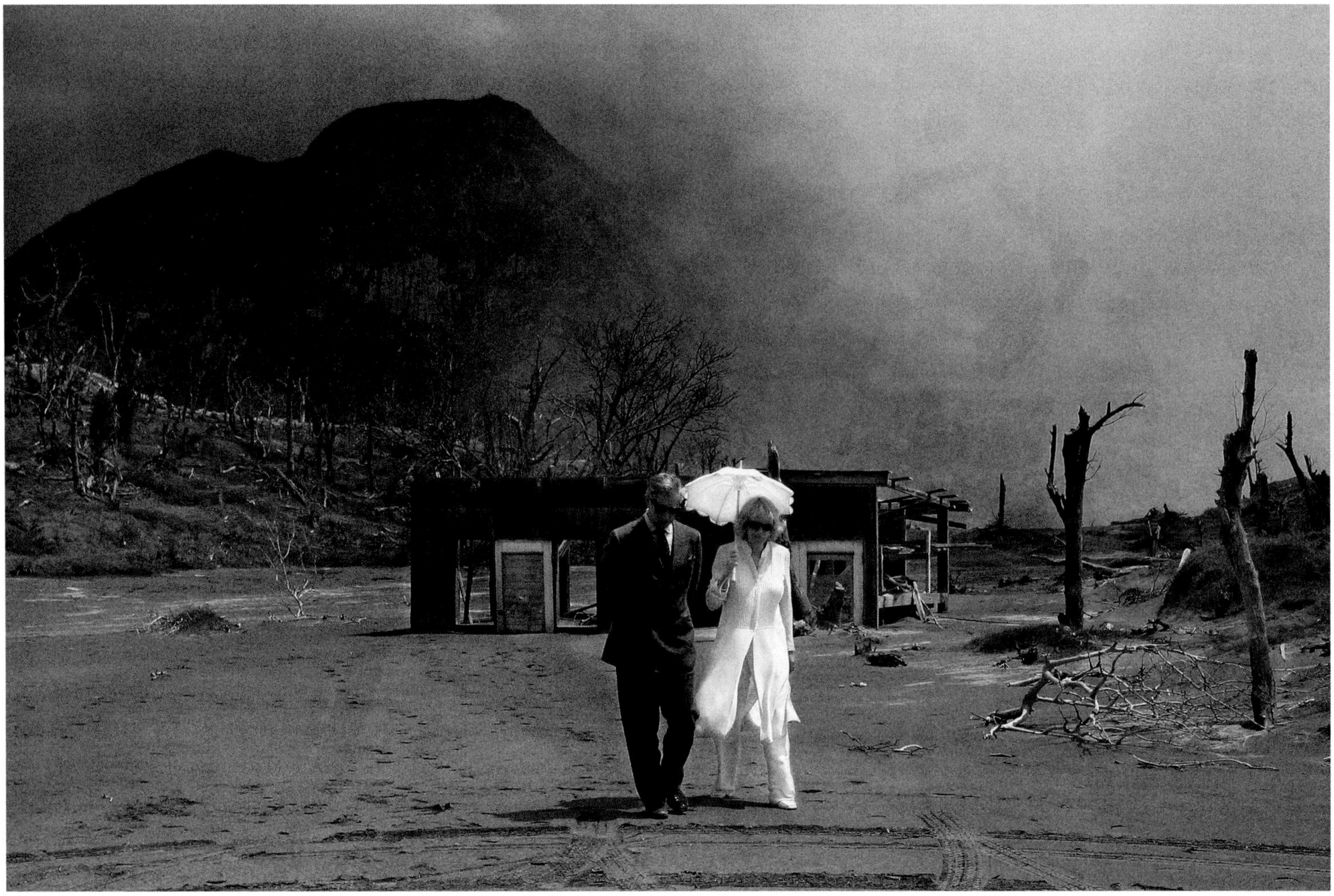

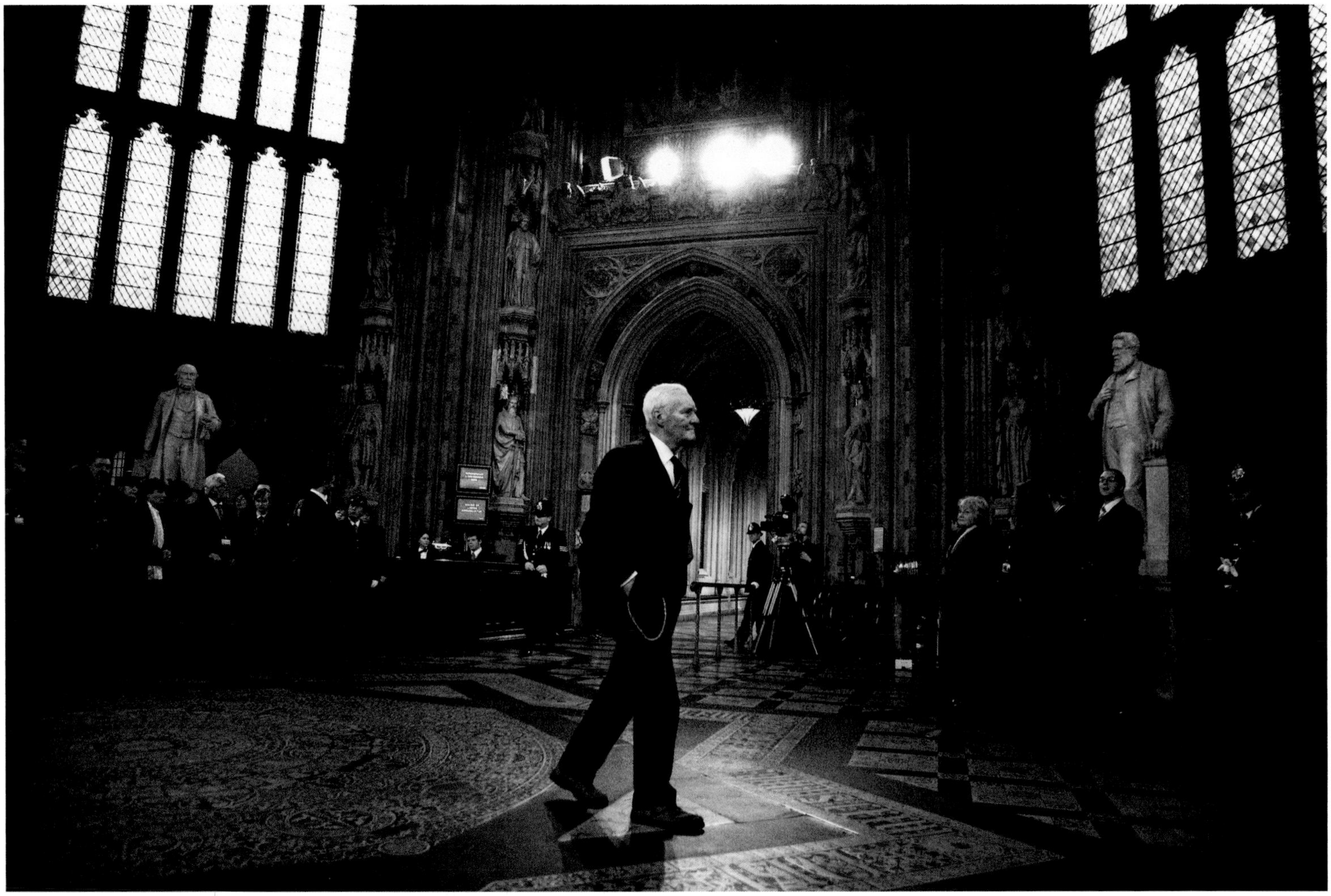

Lewis Whyld PRESS ASSOCIATION
Their Royal Highnesses the Prince of Wales and the Duchess of Cornwall walk through an area devastated by The Soufrière Hills volcano, near Plymouth on the Caribbean island of Montserrat. After a long period of dormancy the volcano, seen behind the Royal couple, became active in 1995 and has erupted numerous times since, destroying the island's capital, Plymouth, and rendering more than half of Montserrat uninhabitable. 8th March 2008

David Sandison THE INDEPENDENT
Britain's foremost socialist Tony Benn still stalks the passages of the Houses of Parliament in Westminster, London. He retired from Parliament in 2001, in his words to 'spend more time involved in politics', suggesting that for him 'real politics' is about struggle rather than parliamentary procedure. 3rd December 2008

John Giles PRESS ASSOCIATION
Conservative Deputy Leader David Davis arrives to vote after he resigned and forced a by-election in his constituency. 10th July 2008

Adrian Dennis AGENCE FRANCE PRESSE
(Left to right) Prince William, Prince Harry, Princess Anne,
Queen Elizabeth II, Prince Phillip, The Duke of Edinburgh,
Camilla, Duchess of Cornwall and Charles, Prince of
Wales watch a flypast from the balcony of Buckingham
Palace Following the Queen's Birthday Parade in
London. The ceremony of Trooping the Colour is
believed to have first been performed during the reign
of King Charles II, and since 1748, has marked the official
birthday of the Sovereign. More than 600 guardsmen
and cavalry make up the parade, a celebration of the
Sovereign's official birthday, although the Queen's
actual birthday is on 21st April. 14th June 2008

Following spread
First Prize: Sports Action
First Prize: Sports Folio of the Year
First Prize: Olympic Folio
First Prize: Olympic Singles
Tom Jenkins THE GUARDIAN
Usain Bolt of Jamaica realises he has won the Olympic men's 200m final with a new world record time of 19.30 seconds. National Stadium, Beijing, China.
20th August 2008

First Prize: Sports Folio of the Year
Tom Jenkins THE GUARDIAN
Stoke City v. Leicester City, Coca-Cola championship
match, Brittiania Stadium, Stoke-on-Trent. Celebrations
at the final whistle as Stoke gain promotion to the
Premier League and Leicester are relegated to League
One. 4th May 2008

First Prize: Sports Folio of the Year
Tom Jenkins THE GUARDIAN
Manchester United v. Barcelona, the Champions League
semi-final 2nd leg match at Old Trafford, Manchester.
Patrice Evra (left) gets an elbow and boot on the chin
from Cristiano Ronaldo (top) and Deco (bottom).
29th April 2008

Dave Shopland
Manchester United v. Chelsea, the Champions League
final. Michael Ballack and his teammates react as their
skipper John Terry misses the penalty that would have
won the cup. 21st May 2008

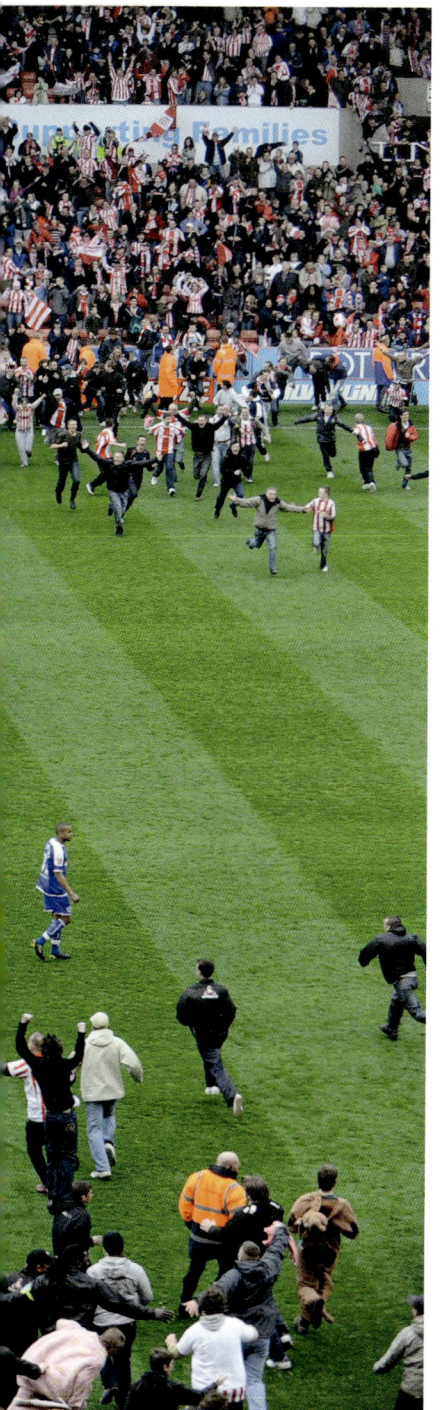

Following spread
First Prize: Sports Folio Of The Year
Tom Jenkins THE GUARDIAN
England v. South Africa rugby union match at
Twickenham Stadium, London. Phil Vickery (centre)
is tackled by Tendai Mtawarira (right) while he hands
off Victor Matfield (left) in the eye. 22nd November 2008

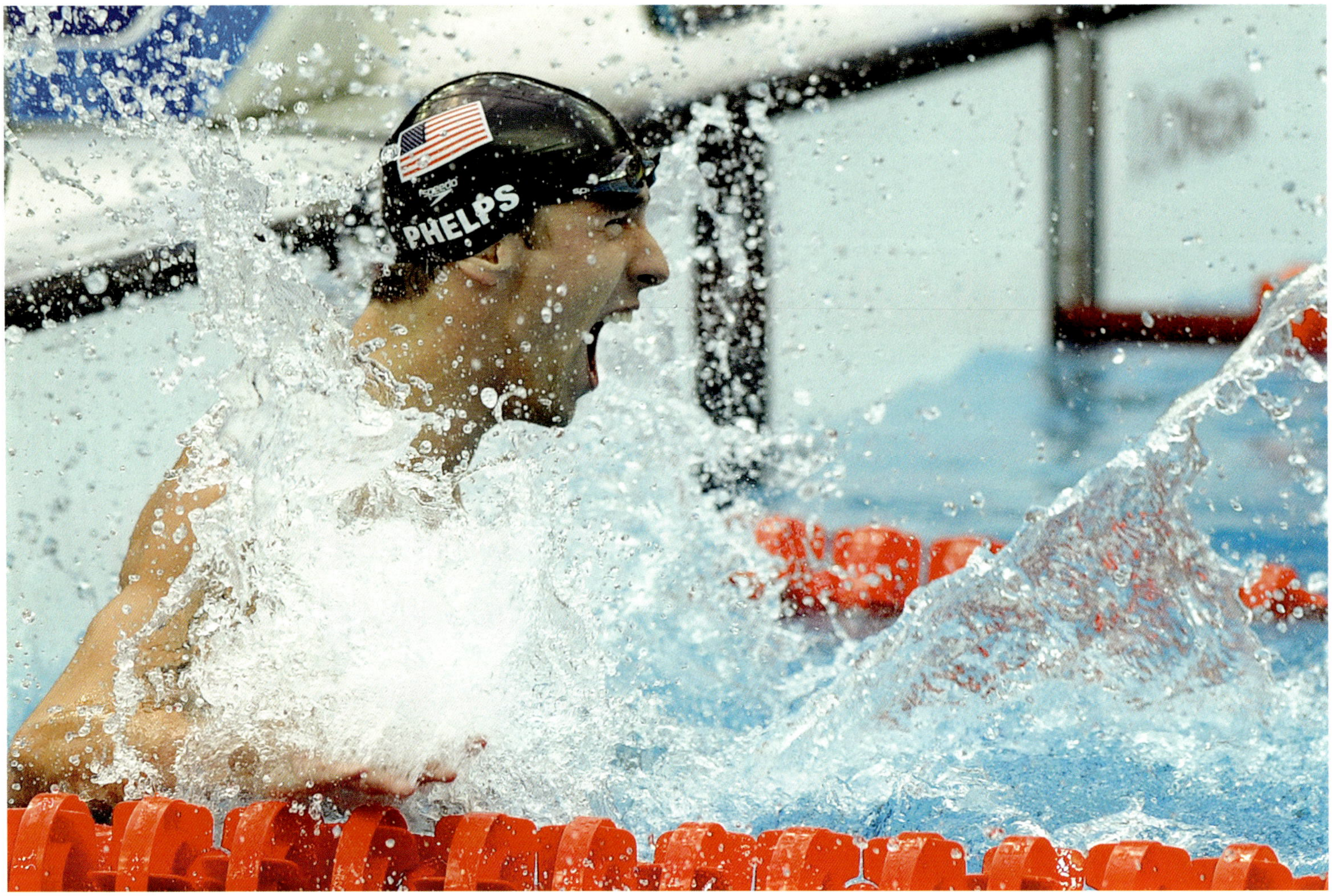
PHELPS

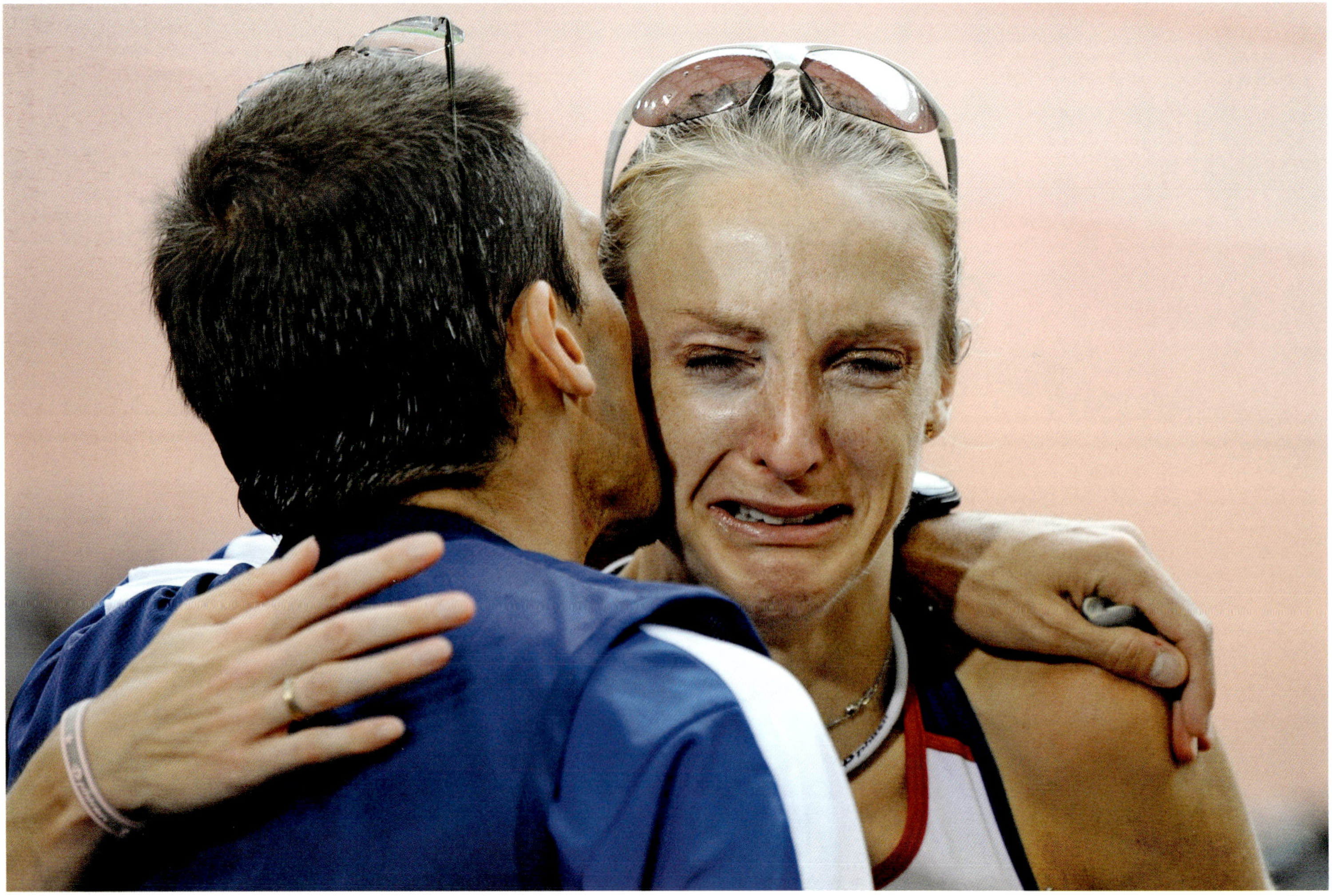

Clive Mason GETTY IMAGES
Jean-Baptiste Grange of France in action on the
downhill section of the super combined event of
the Mens FIS Ski World Cup in Val d'Isere, France.
3rd February 2008

Stewart Harrison SWINDON ADVERTISER
Jockey Rachael Green is thrown from her horse,
Barney's Mate, at the Barbury Castle point-to-point.
12th January 2008

Roger Federer (right) and Stanislas Wawrinka of Switzerland celebrate after defeating Thomas Johansson and Simon Aspelin of Sweden during the men's doubles gold medal tennis match at the Beijing Olympic Games. 16th August 2008

Rafael Nadal celebrates at match point in the final against David Ferrer during the Open Sabadell Atlantico tournament at the Real Club in Barcelona, Spain. 4th May 2008

Liezel Huber (left) of USA and Cara Black of Zimbabwe in action during the ladies' doubles quarter-final match against Victoria Azarenka of Belarus and Shahar Peer of Israel during the Wimbledon Lawn Tennis Championships in London. 2nd July 2008

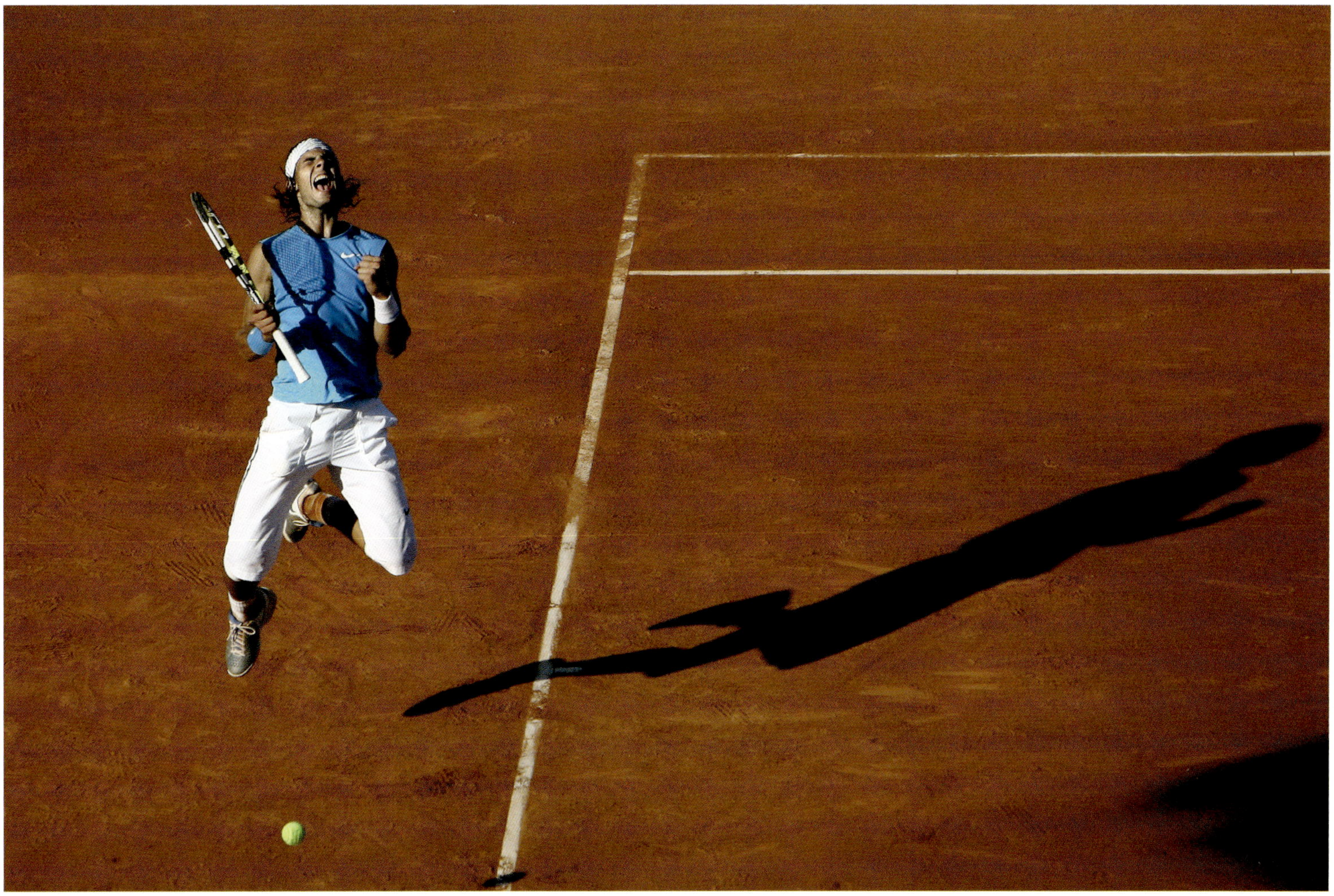

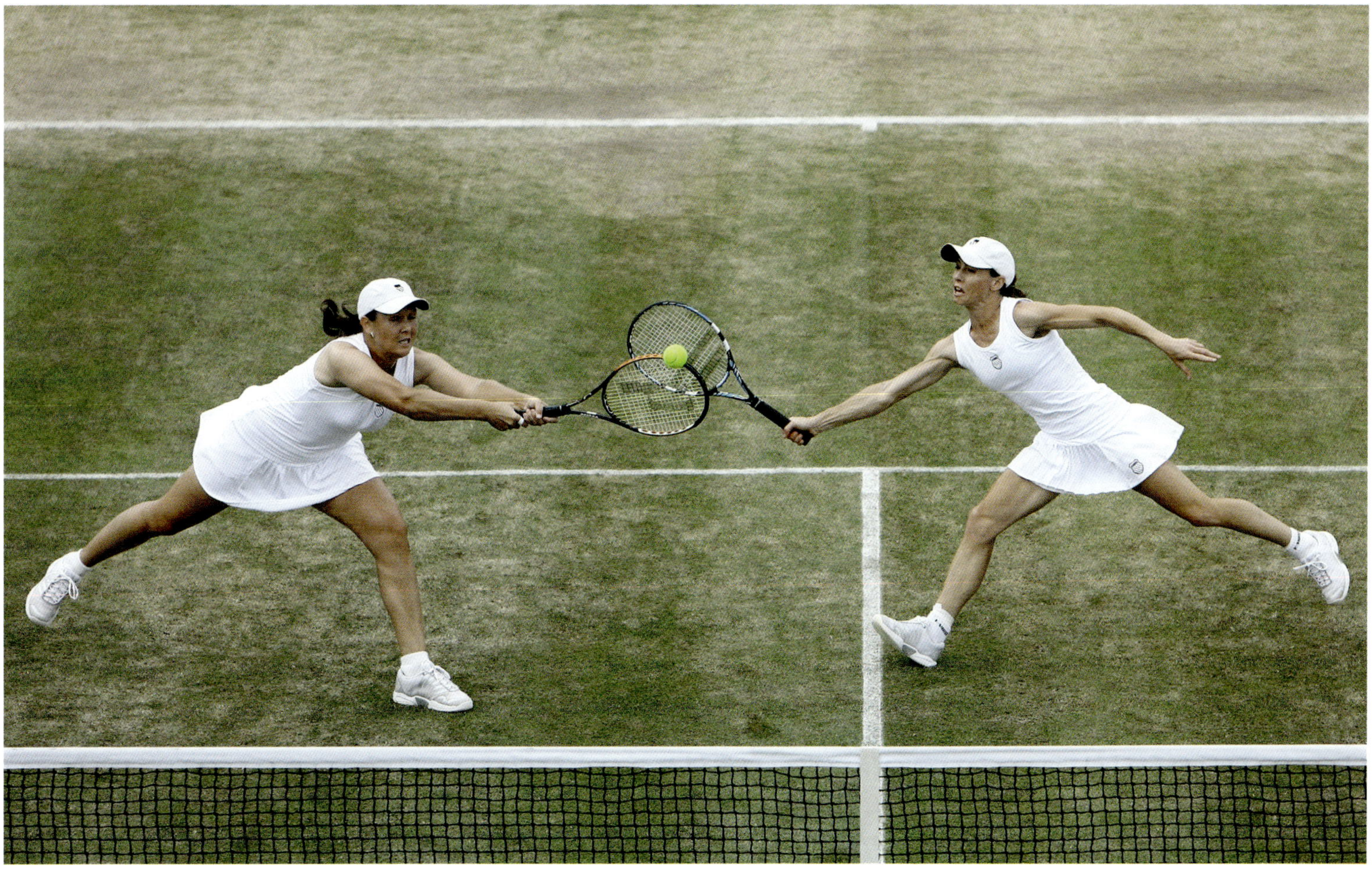

Graham Chadwick DAILY MAIL
Rafael Nadal celebrates with the crowd after defeating
Roger Federer in the marathon 4 hour 48 minute men's
singles final at Wimbledon. 6th July 2008

Felipe Trueba Garcia URPA
Rafael Nadal with the winner's trophy, following his
victory over Roger Federer in their men's singles final at
Wimbledon. It ended in near darkness on the Centre
Court after 4 hours and 48 minutes. 6th July 2008

Richard Pelham THE SUN
The Liverpool skipper Stephen Gerrard celebrates
his team's progression to the quarter-finals of the
Champions League after beating Inter Milan 3-0
on aggregate. 11th March 2008

Richard Heathcote GETTY IMAGES
Gonzalo Fernandez-Castano of Spain celebrates
in the lake around the 18th green after beating Lee
Westwood in a play-off during the final round of the
Quinn Insurance British Masters on The Brabazon
course at The Belfry near Sutton Coldfield, England.
28th September 2008

Eddie Keogh REUTERS
Lewis Hamilton celebrates as he drives past his pit crew
after winning the British F1 Grand Prix at the Silverstone
circuit in England. 6th July 2008

Clive Mason GETTY IMAGES
New Formula One World Champion Lewis Hamilton
celebrates taking the championship by a single point
Following the Brazilian Grand Prix at the Interlagos
Circuit, Sao Paulo, Brazil. 2nd November 2008

Paul Gilham GETTY IMAGES
McLaren Mercedes driver Lewis Hamilton is seen in his
garage during practice for the German Grand Prix at the
Hockenheimring, Germany. 18th July 2008

Clive Mason GETTY IMAGES
Sunbathers relax as Lewis Hamilton drives by during
practice for the Monaco Grand Prix at the Monte Carlo
Circuit in Monaco. 22nd May 2008

Following spread
Michael Steele GETTY IMAGES
Ricky Ponting and Matthew Hayden of Australia lie on
the ground along with the Indian players and umpire
Billy Bowden as a swarm of bees pass over the ground
during day three of the Third Test match between India
and Australia at the Feroz Shah Kotla Stadium in New
Delhi, India. 31st October 2008

09 | 10

The Press Photographer's Year

The Press Photographer's Year would like to thank all the photographers who submitted photographs for the competition and for kindly allowing us to reproduce them in this book and at the accompanying exhibition.

The copyright for each of the photographs published in this book is held by the individual photographer, with the exception of the following publications and agencies:

The Press Photographer's Year are very grateful to them for their permissions.

Agence France Presse; 62, 77 bottom
Associated Press; 88
Daily Mail; 29, 74
Evening Standard; 25 bottom
Getty Images; 18, 20 both, 21 both, 22, 25 top, 30, 32, 33, 34, 35, 38, 58 both, 59, 67, 71, 92, 96, 97, 98, 103, 106 both, 107, 108, 109, 110, 111, 112, 114, 116, 117
The Guardian; 54, 118
Irish Independent 39, 80
Pacemaker Press; 75, 78
Press Association; 24, 70, 72, 77 top, 87, 90, 104
Presseye; 36
Reuters; 14, 26, 52, 91
South West News Service; 48, 76
Sunday Tribune; 12, 15
The Times; 53, 83 top, 100

All the copyright holders have asserted their moral rights under the UK Copyright Designs & Patents Act 1988.

The Press Photographer's Year would not have been possible without the generous support of Canon Cameras. We would like to thank Matt Beard at Canon UK for his dedication to the project.

We would also like to thank the following people for their time, their support and valuable assistance during The Press Photographer's Year.

2010 Jury
Roger Allen (Chairman)
Philip Coburn
Jez Coulson
Nic Dunlop
Rosie Hallam
Graham Trott
Neil Turner

2010 Multimedia Jury
Dan Chung (Chairman)
Rodney Charters ASC
Dr D J Clark
Kate Pattison
Adam Westbrook

2010 Sports Jury
Tom Jenkins (Chairman)
Stuart MacFarlane

at TalkingPixels.co.uk
Tom Scott, James Crossett, Zbyszek Zemla

at SMITH
Stuart Smith, Victoria Forrest, Selina Swayne, Namkwan Cho

at the National Theatre
John Langley, Alison Chown, Caroline Ansdell

at Passavia, Passau
Elmar Steubl, Michael Wallrapp, Sandra Kössl

at Loxley Colour, Glasgow
Christopher Kay, Robert Orr, Audrey Smith

a special vote of thanks must go to
Alastair Mackeown
Brian Murphy & Nigel Learmond

thanks also to
Hazel Dunlop, Stuart Morcom, Victoria Routledge, Allan Titmuss,

A major exhibition of the photographs from this book was held at the National Theatre on London's South Bank between 10th July and 10th September 2010 was designed by SMITH, printed by Loxley Colour and sponsored by Canon.

Published by the PPY PRESS
Press Photographers Year Ltd.
47 Moore Park Road
London SW6 2HP
call us: +44(0)20 3239 9908
email us: info@theppy.com
visit us: www.theppy.com

Produced by Dillon Bryden & Tim Bishop
Collated by Dillon Bryden & Neil Turner
Design: SMITH, Victoria Forrest, Selina Swayne
www.smith-design.com

Printing & Repro: Passavia, Passau

Printed in Germany on Profi Silk 170 gsm and Invercote G 300 gsm acid-free papers.

ISBN 978-0-9556019-2-7

10

The Press Photographer's Year

Photograph of the Year
David Bebber THE TIMES
The Libyan leader Colonel Gaddafi stands behind
protective glass during a military parade in Green
Square, Tripoli held to celebrate his 40 years as
head of state. 1st September 2009

Foreword
Roger Allen
Chairman of the 2010 Jury

This year's Chairman of the Jury, Roger Allen, has been on the staff of the Mirror for over 24 years, travelling all over the world covering many of the big news stories of the last few decades. Tim Bishop caught up with him as he was completing a five-day Hostile Environment training course down in Reading.

Tim Bishop Just how hard was it to reduce the 7,500 entries down to just an edit of 120, and decide on category winners?

Roger Allen Pure volume makes the judging very difficult. I wonder if we need a weeding-out process before it goes before the panel of judges, but I guess everyone does have the right to be judged. First we have the slide show, which gives us all an immediate feel for the best pictures; they really do jump out from the crowd. So that the first thirty pictures or so we all agreed on. After that it's much harder to agree when we get down to the last seven, they're all very strong images. I think judging is helped by having a good eye for a picture. When you push the button yourself, you know straight away 'Christ, that's a good picture!' It's almost a tingle you get, and it's the same feeling when you see an image either on the slide show, or as a hard copy print - you know straight away in your bones it's a good picture.

TB Do you have some favourite images from the competition this year?

RA David Levene's photograph of the handcart in Haiti piled with the corpses is a truly great picture. It has a timeless quality to it; nothing there makes it a modern day scene. David Bebber's picture of Gaddafi and all the reflections in the glass won our 'Photograph of the Year' and I remember as soon as I saw it that I thought, 'I wish I'd taken that.' Gaddafi is in a world of his own, even though he is covered with all those medals and ribbons and is in his elaborate uniform. It was a fantastic picture that just didn't fit into any category. It had to be the 'Photograph of the Year', even though it didn't win any of the other categories.

TB What would you say makes a great news photographer?

RA The key qualities are tenacity, like a Jack Russell terrier, and awkwardness. Getting the great picture is the combination of everything you hoped and dreamed of coming together in front of your lens to produce a winner. It's the 'perfect storm', when it all just falls into place. That ability to see where the 'perfect storm' could happen comes with experience. Great photographers look at getting into just the right position where they think the Great Picture might happen, being devious, wily with absolute determination to get the very best image. There are always some who just happen to be in the right place and at the right time, but the best they are likely to ever get is the one-off picture. There are a few great photographers working, and it is the same names that come up again and again. They've got themselves into the right position, and get those great pictures over and over again.

TB Which photographers inspired you when you started on newspapers?

RA I most admired Terry Fincher, a legendary staff photographer from the Express (a founder member of The BPPA). I have just been looking at a new book of photographs from Henri Cartier-Bresson. It's fascinating to see how he travelled, very different from today where only last week I was in Borneo for only a few days for a job with a reporter, then straight home again. Cartier-Bresson took a patchwork of planes, ships, and local transport to remote places where he would spend three months taking rolls and rolls of film before bringing it all back with him.

TB Where do you think our industry is going?

RA It's getting progressively smaller; the pool of photographers is reducing. The work being carried out by the staffers and dedicated pool of freelance photographers is great, but it's up against 800 pictures from the agencies every time. Take Obama's visit to London, a staff photographer's chances of getting pictures into their paper was almost nil as almost everyone there submitted their work on a no use, no fee basis. Photographic standards might be higher, but newspapers will eventually stop employing their own staff, as they know they'll get images from the agencies.

When I joined the Mirror twenty-four years ago, there were thirty-five staff photographers, there are nine now, and by this September it will be down to three. PA, Reuters, Getty and AP are covering a far higher range of news jobs. Picture editors are now using their staff for in-house feature jobs on sections like property and lifestyle rather than on news jobs. As a result we're not really shooting a lot that would look good in these awards.

I was astonished a couple of years ago attending a very ordinary job at Madame Tussauds to photograph Jose Mourinho unveiling a waxwork of himself. I thought there might be four others there. There were over 60 photographers, and only three others I recognised from national papers. I've never seen those pictures published anywhere. What happened to all the photographs those teams of photographers took? Where did they publish and crucially, who paid for them to be there and how do they make a living?

Introduction
Tim Bishop
Co-Founder of The Press Photographer's Year

It would be a hard act to follow. The previous speaker had shown pictures of scantily clad models on some Caribbean island. The Canon invited audience had listened in awe as he described his 'glamour' photography. My brief was to talk about the winning entries in the Press Photographer's Year awards.

But in the way of touring lectures, the audience adapts to the presenter, and I saw the older male crowd, sated by tanned bikini images, drift out as I got to my feet. A younger, scruffier, more mixed crew fill in to take their vacated seats. And in the way of photography students, this new crowd were big on the key asks: How to do it, or more specifically 'how can I do it'. So the presentation began to change. They wanted to go to war. So I found myself steered away from Canon cameras and how they have stood behind us in this hard time of recession, giving back to photographers in generous sponsorship of our competition, even away from the great photography shown in the PPY. It was because my crowd wanted to be out covering the biggest story of their decade. The War on Terror.

Well I've been there. Though a while ago now. And it's hard to admit to this reverent young attractive and rapt audience that I just wasn't very good. Sent to cover conflict around the world, including the first Gulf war, when I worked for The Times, I found to my surprise, that I really wasn't very good at war.

I was scared for a start, which is unhelpful. The people who are really good just don't seem to register fear in the way I did. Under fire, I forgot 'the decisive moment' and just wanted to hide. The places I was sent by my eager picture desk, snugly from the offices in Wapping, East London included Kuwait, Israel, and Northern Ireland, yet we always arrived after the event, witnessing the mess, or lurked about waiting for something vile to happen. I remember my reporter and I hiding in a dark basement in a northern Israeli border town as Soviet made rockets thudded into the ground above our heads. No pictures, no great spreads in the making, just simple raw fear and swinging dim light bulb in a ceiling.

So in front of this crowd, I spoke not of photography, but about loss. My lasting experience of war has been the loss of friends. And my key warning to these ranks of budding war photographers is that they may die. I didn't take too many images that will last in the memory, like so many of the pictures in this book. But I did take some of the risks. Good, gifted, wonderful press photographers I knew and treasured took the risks too. Too many have died, but here are just two I think of most days even now.

Alan Harper was killed covering the same story as me. He was a man who was about as an unlikely a war photographer as can be.

A staff photographer with the Financial Times, he was more accustomed to boardrooms than the debris of conflict. He died photographing the capping of the burning Kuwaiti oil fields, ignited by retreating Iraqi soldiers in 1991.

Only three years earlier in 1989, my very great friend Ian Parry, who once drove all the way from Madrid to join me on another story in Gibraltar so that we could have a drink together at the Rock Hotel, was killed on assignment in Romania as the iron curtain fell around Eastern Europe. He was only 24.

But it's not just the dead that stick in my mind. I think of those who so recently had a lucky escape, though not without serious injury. Two years ago, the Irish photographer John D McHugh, who started his career as a DJ in Dublin bars, graduating from shifts on the Guardian, to a contract with the French agency AFP, found himself embedded with US forces fighting in Kunar province, Afghanistan. Days into his assignment, a high velocity round struck him in the stomach. At last years Press Photographer's Year Awards, John chatted happily at the reception, yet his t-shirt fitted in a strange way over his chest, as if he were an incompetent shoplifter that had attempted to hide his plunder carelessly. This was the legacy of the countless abdominal procedures that saved his life. Then this January, on my birthday, came the news that a freelance press photographer working in Afghanistan had been seriously injured and his reporter killed in a bomb explosion. I was standing in Tesco's in Fulham. I froze. The name of the photographer was a man whose work I had not only admired for over a decade, but was a great friend, someone I had worked closely with at the Telegraph for many years.

His reporter Rupert Hamer, the defence correspondent of the Daily Mirror, died at the scene, but he survived, losing the lower part of both his limbs. Bravely, he is making a spirited recovery, using artificial legs, and as part of that accepted our invitation to be part of the jury for this year's competition, adding his powerful, outspoken, uncompromising views into the mix. He is Phil Coburn. I have a strange feeling we'll be seeing his byline again soon.

Following spread
David Levene
A man walks past a barrow laden with corpses at the Grande Cemetiere in Port-au-Prince, four days after the earthquake that struck Haiti on 12th January 2010. Death toll estimates following the disaster have ranged between 170,000 and 250,000 and in the days immediately after the earthquake so many dead bodies were dumped here that they ended up strewn throughout the avenues and walkways of the cemetery. Most unidentified bodies were eventually buried in mass graves around the edges of the city. 16th January 2010

David Levene
The father of a child lying injured reads a small bible in an outdoor compound of the Jean Damien Childrens Hospital near to the American Embassy in Port-Au-Prince. Previously only admitting patients up to the age of 18, the hospital opened its doors to both children and adults in an effort to treat as many people as possible that were injured in the earthquake. 16th January 2010

David Levene
Young men trade tyres recently scavenged from a nearby ruined building on Rue Pavee in downtown Port-Au-Prince. So called 'looting' was generally over-reported by international media. Although there were pockets of looting activity in a small area of downtown Port-au-Prince, the scenes around the wider city were of people calmly trying to continue with their lives in the face of horrendous disaster and destruction. 20th January 2010

Ben Gurr THE TIMES
Desperate survivors of the massive earthquake in Haiti collect sacks of rice from a World Food Programme distribution point in Port Au Prince. 26th January 2010

Following spread
Mark Condren SUNDAY TRIBUNE
A man stands at the ruin of a church after the
earthquake struck Haiti. 26th January 2010

First Prize: Features

Dylan Martinez REUTERS
A dog walker strolls through an earthquake-damaged district of Padang in Indonesia's West Sumatra province. 7th October 2009

Mark Condren SUNDAY TRIBUNE
A boy walking with his bicycle tyre in Uganda.
21st October 2009

Adam Dean PANOS
US Army Soldier Sgt. Baker from Viper Company 126,
1st Platoon, directs artillery after being hit by 10 RPGs
at Restrepo Firebase in the restive Korengal Valley close
to the Pakistan border in Kunar Province of Afghanistan.
8th March 2009

Adam Dean PANOS
US Army Soldiers from Viper Company 126, 2nd Platoon,
fire 120mm mortars during an attack on Restrepo
Firebase in the restive Korengal Valley close to the
Pakistan border in Kunar Province of Afghanistan.
21st March 2009

Following spread

Daniel Berehulak GETTY IMAGES

10 year old Nawab Mian, who suffers from mental illness, plays with a small chick near the site of the deserted Union Carbide factory in Bhopal, India. 28th November 2009

Following spread

Daniel Berehulak GETTY IMAGES

Nafiza Bee, co-ordinator of the Chingari Trust Clinic carrying 8 year old Annan who suffers from cerebral palsy and receives vital rehabilitative support and care at the clinic near Bhopal. 27th November 2009

Daniel Berehulak GETTY IMAGES

Ground water, believed to be contaminated, at a village near the Union Carbide factory in Bhopal. 27th November 2009

Daniel Berehulak GETTY IMAGES

15 year old Sachin Kumar crawls on his hands and knees after playing a game of cricket with his friends in a slum near the site of the deserted Union Carbide factory in Bhopal. Sachin was born with a birth defect rendering his legs practically useless. He had been receiving physical therapy treatment and education from the Chingari Trust rehabilitation Centre for victims of the 1984 gas tragedy but his health has turned for the worse and his legs, now covered with open sores, restrict him from travelling to the place where a bus can pick him up for daily treatment. 27th November 2009

Daniel Berehulak GETTY IMAGES

Children play in front of their homes in a village near the Union Carbide factory in Bhopal. 29th November 2009

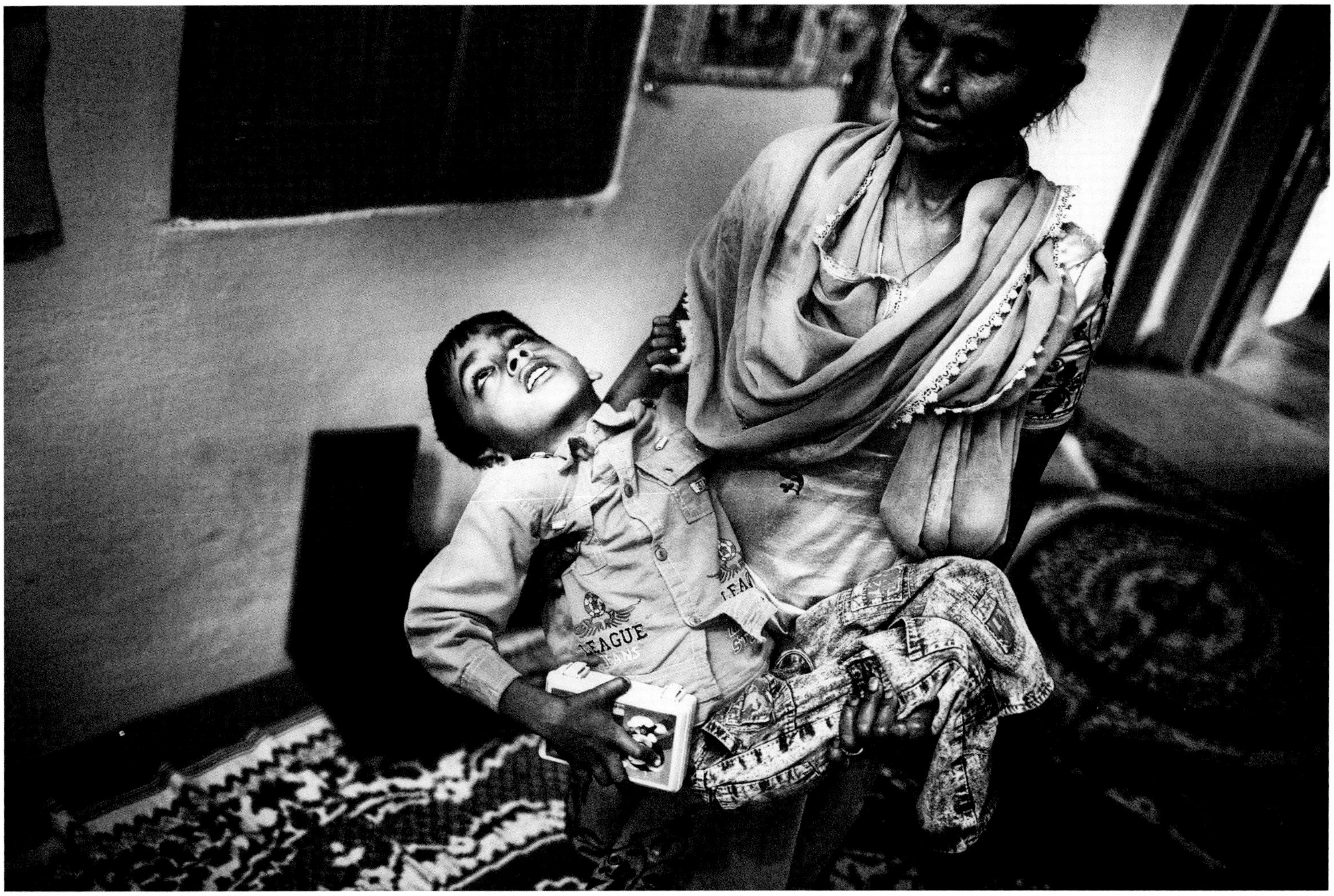
LEAGUE

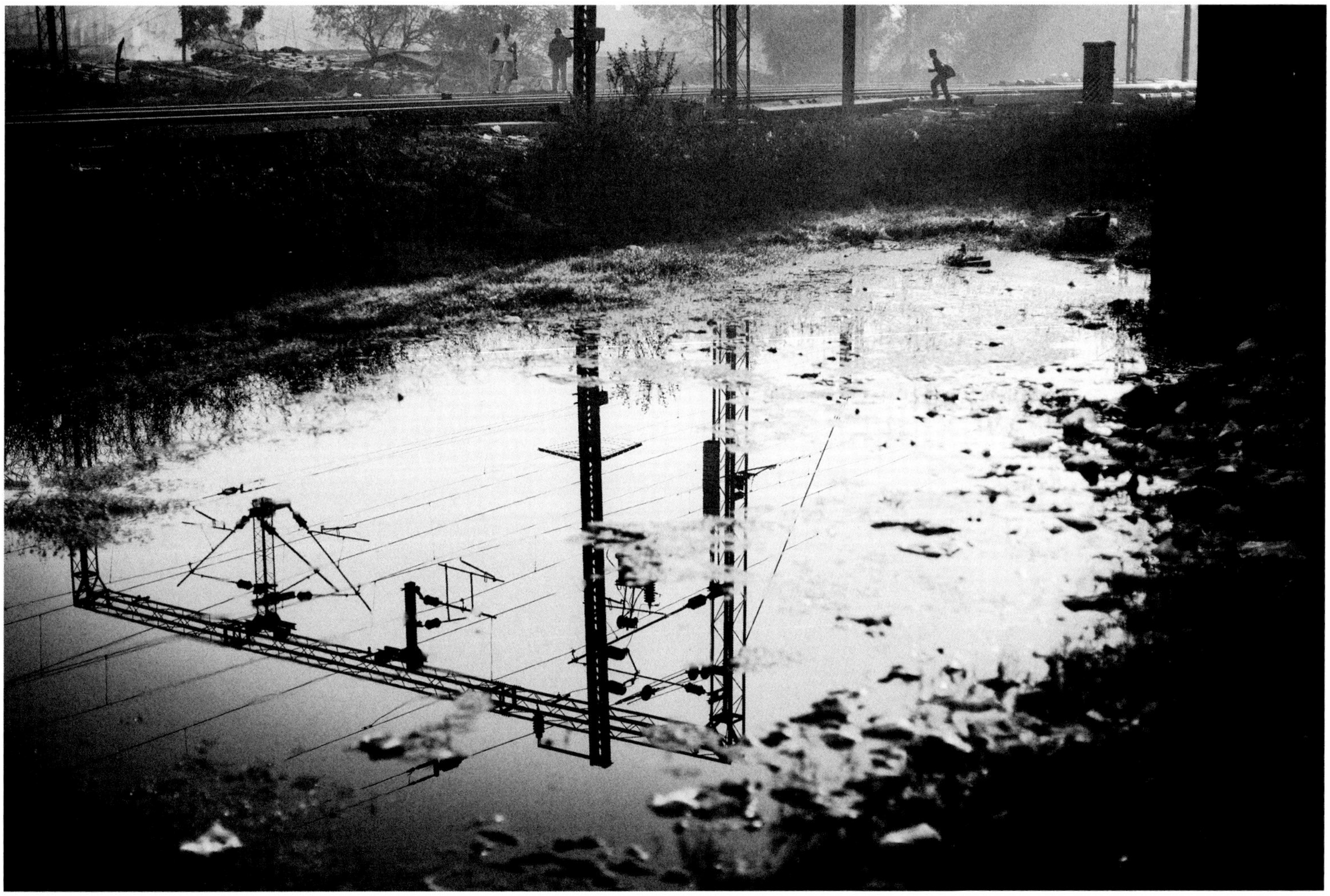

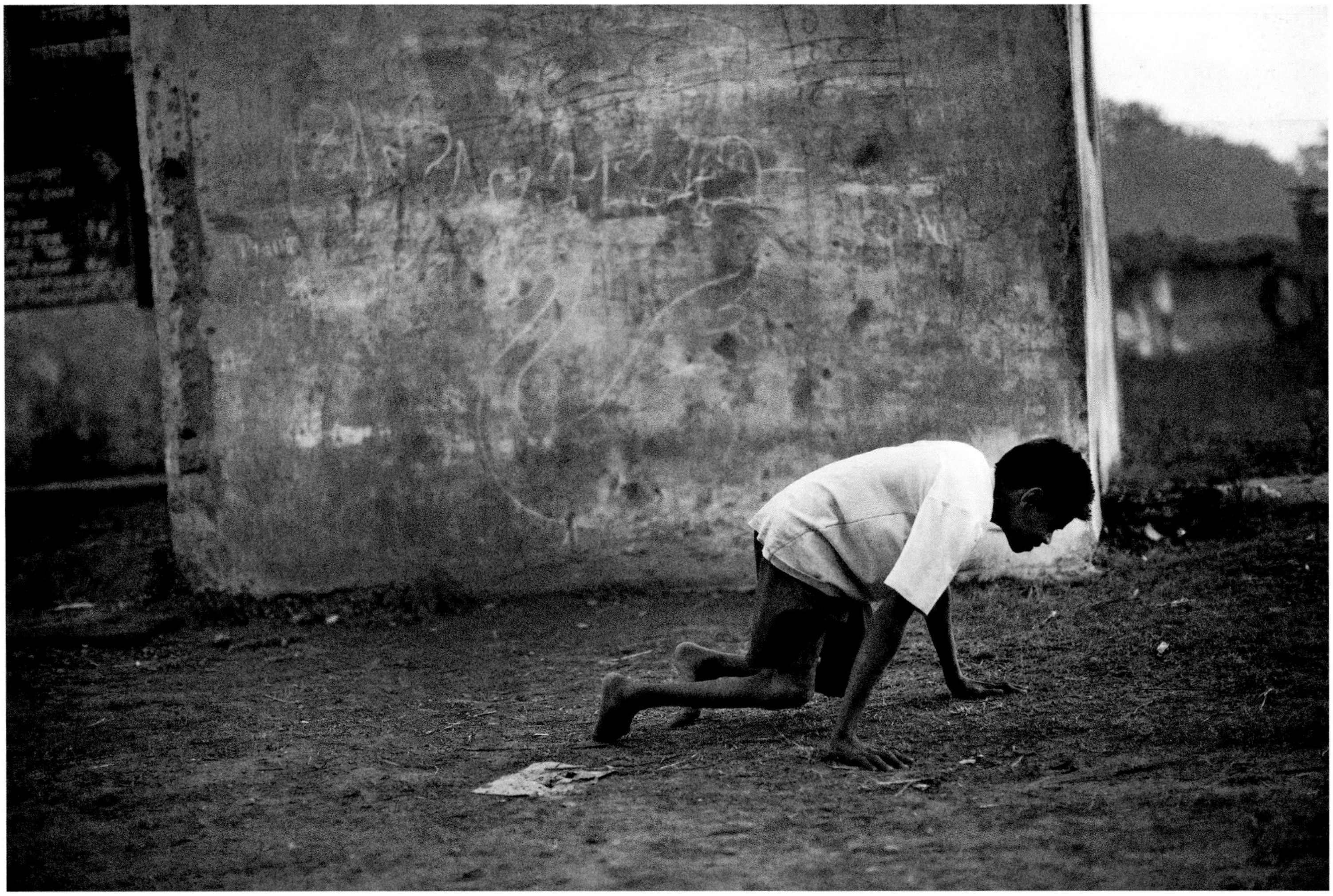

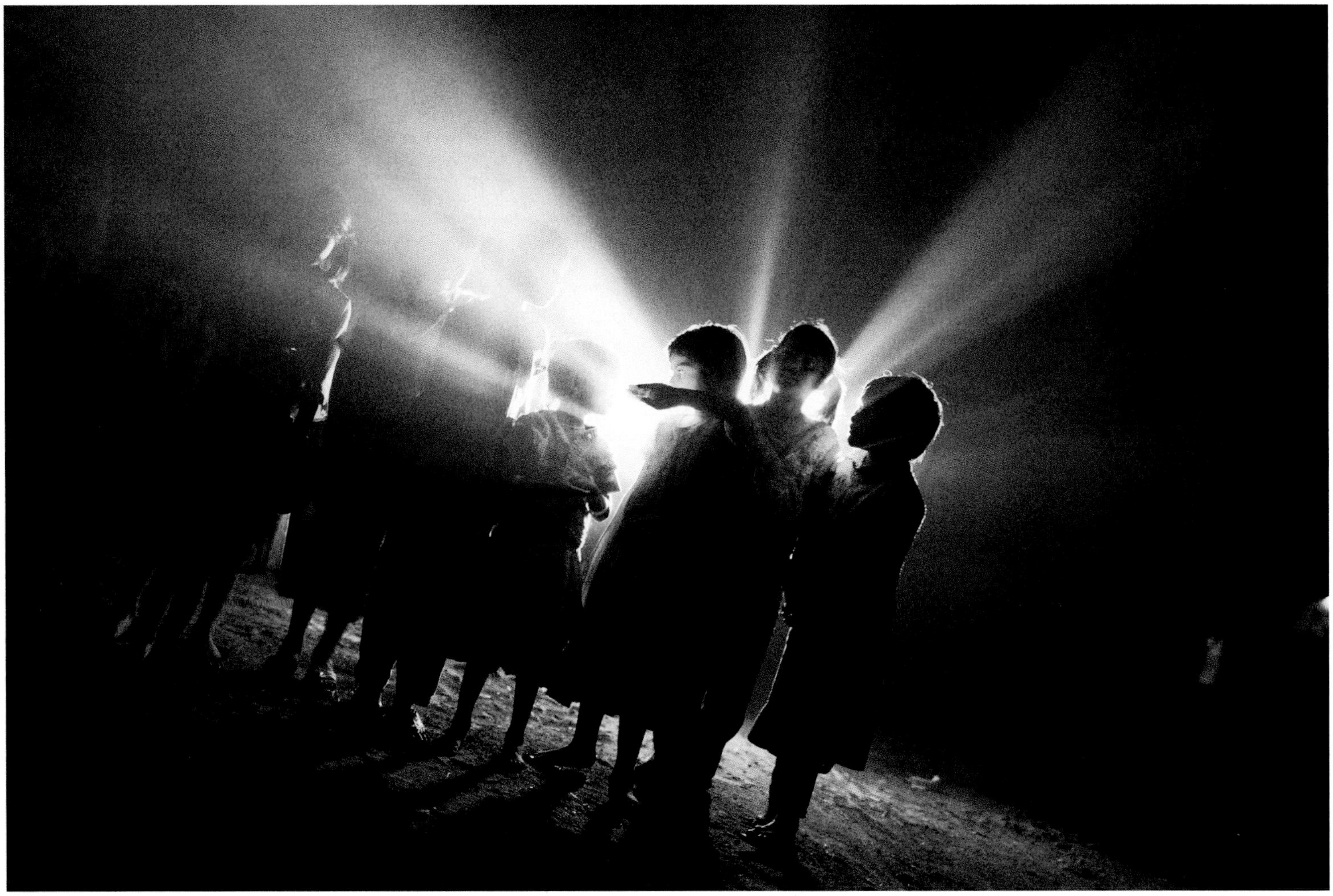

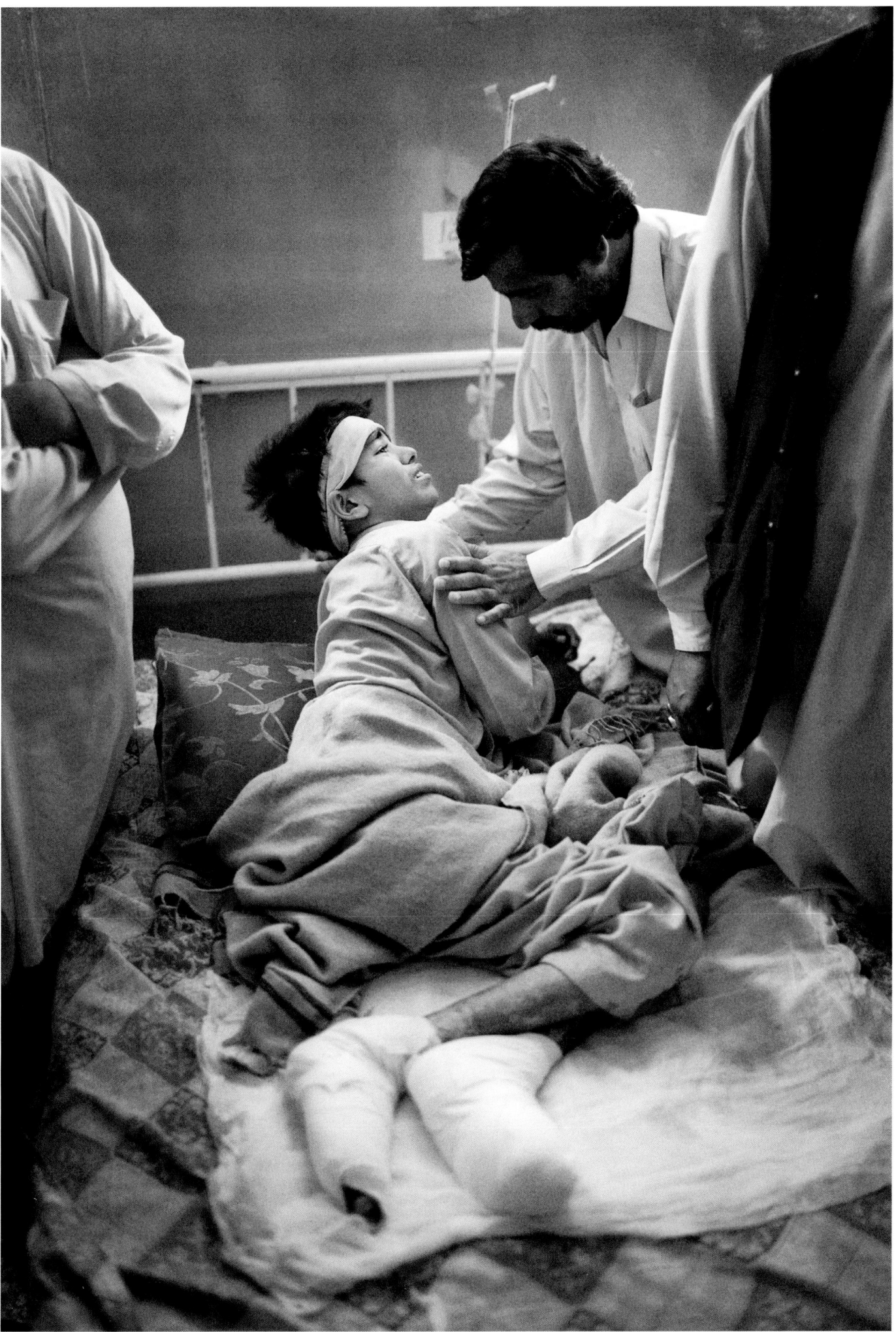

Daniel Berehulak GETTY IMAGES

13 year old Pakhtoum Kumar being consoled by a neighbour at a hospital in Mardan, north west Pakistan. He lost the toes on one foot and has injuries to his other as a result of shelling by the Pakistan military in his village of Mata in Swat. 9th May 2009

Kieran Dodds PANOS

A 40 year old mother and her 12 year old daughter admitted to the Poipet Clinic in Cambodia which has the second highest HIV rate in Asia. Poipet, on the border with Thailand, is a major source of infection from sex tourists, trafficking and poor education. Dependants will usually spend time with their parents in the hospital helping to care for them. 20th November 2009

John Giles PRESS ASSOCIATION
The Cap and medals of bomb disposal officer Loren Marlton Thomas who was killed while serving in Afghanistan are given to his family following his burial at Lytham Cemetry. 8th December 2009

Dan Kitwood GETTY IMAGES
Friends and family react as the hearses carrying the coffins of six dead soldiers pass mourners lining the High Street in Wootton Bassett. Warrant Officer Darren Chant 40, Sergeant Matthew Telford 37, Guardsman James Major 18, of 1st Battalion, The Grenadier Guards, Acting Corporal Steven Boote 22, and Corporal Nicholas Webster-Smith, both of the Royal Military Police were killed as a result of gunshot wounds sustained in an attack at a police checkpoint in the Nad e-Ali district of Helmand province on 3rd November 2009. Sergeant Phillip Scott from 3rd Battalion, The Rifles, who was killed on 5th November 2009, was also repatriated. 10th November 2009

Jeremy Selwyn EVENING STANDARD
Repatriation service for three dead servicemen in Wootten Basett. 18th August 2009

Following spread
First Prize: News
Kieran Doherty REUTERS
A young girl stands with other mourners as the hearses carrying the coffins of five British soldiers are driven through the streets of Wootton Bassett. Lance Sergeant Dave Greenhalgh, Lance Corporal Darren Hicks, Kingsman Sean Dawson, Rifleman Mark Marshall and Sapper Guy Mellors were killed in separate incidents in Afghanistan's Helmand province earlier in the month. 18th February 2009

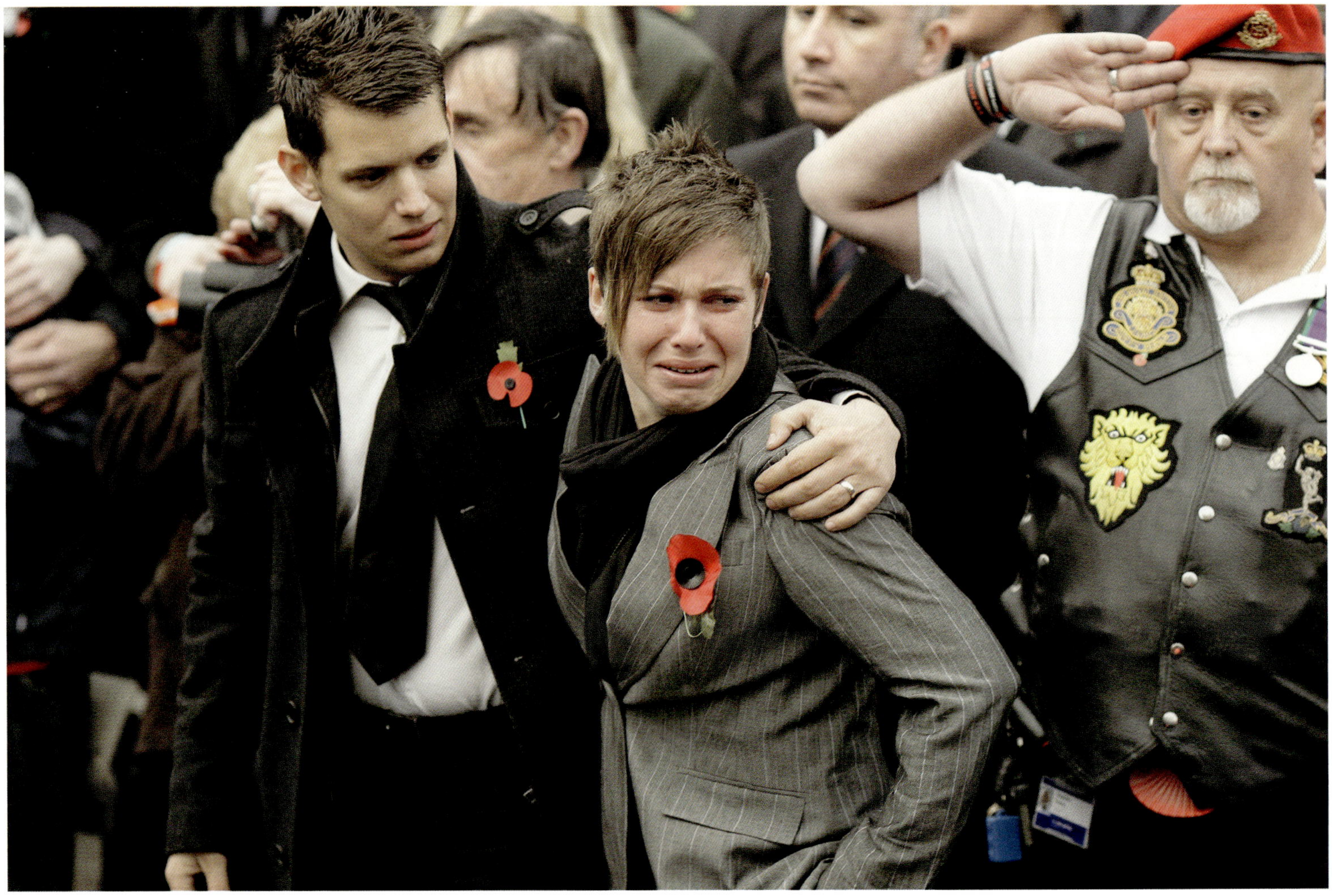

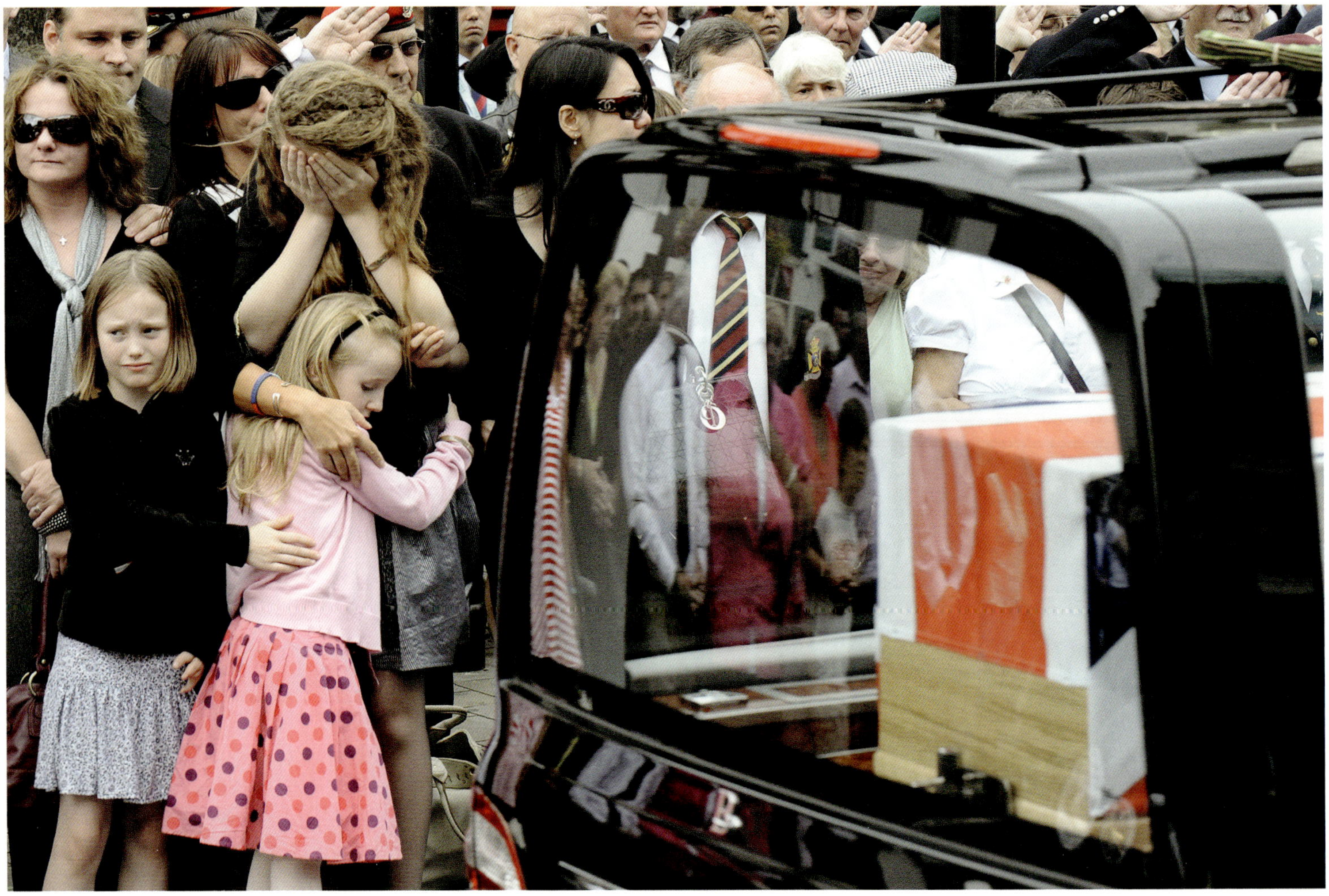

Eamon Ward

Vitaly cares for his fifteen year old daughter Sasha in their one bedroom apartment in the city of Gomel in Southern Belarus. He cares for her during the day and must go to work as a night watchman each evening. Chernobyl's human costs are widespread, affecting about seven million people. A generation later children are still being born with birth defects, heart problems and thyroid cancer. 15th January 2010

Bruce Adams DAILY MAIL

4 year old Harley Slack, who lost both arms and legs after contracting meningitis, being comforted by his parents Samantha Slack and Adam Lane at the Royal Childrens Hospital in Manchester. 24th June 2009

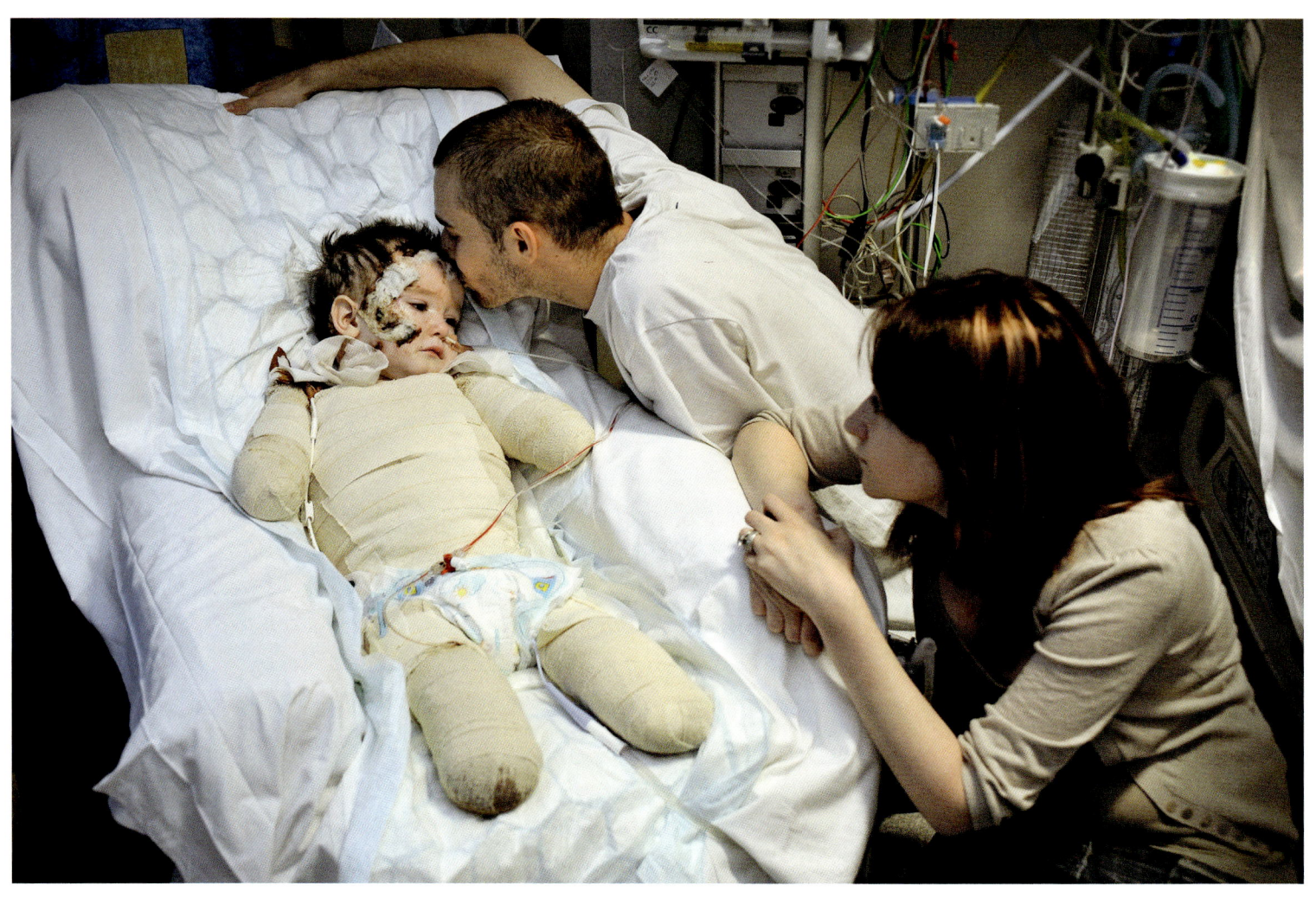

Following spread
First Prize, News Folio
Daniel Berehulak GETTY IMAGES
An Indonesian rescue worker looks on as a team remove debris in an attempt to free dead bodies from rubble in Padang, Indonesia. An earthquake measuring 7.6 struck at 5.16pm local time 85km under the sea to the north-west 3 days earlier. The death toll has exceeded 1,500.
3rd October 2009

First Prize: News Folio
Daniel Berehulak GETTY IMAGES
A PML protester is arrested after being beaten by police in Lahore, Pakistan. Violence had erupted after PML leader Nawaz Sharif defied house arrest, calling for the people of Pakistan to stand up for their rights and continue the long march to Islamabad. Protesters and lawyers clashed with police in the streets as they congregated near to the High Court of Lahore calling for the reinstatement of judges sacked by the previous military president, General Musharraf. 15th March 2009

First Prize: News Folio
Daniel Berehulak GETTY IMAGES
Afghan police drag the bodies of two suspected Taliban killed in a gunfight after they had foiled an attack on a polling station in Kabul. 20th August 2009

First Prize: News Folio
Daniel Berehulak GETTY IMAGES

Indian children work next to their parents at a construction project in front of the Jawaharlal Nehru Stadium in New Delhi. The Commonwealth Games are due to be held in the Indian capital in October 2010 but concerns remain over construction of its sporting and transport infrastructure. The sheer scale of the project has drawn an enormous population of migrant workers from all over India. 30th January 2010

First Prize: News Folio
Daniel Berehulak GETTY IMAGES

A young girl displaced from her home by military operations against the Taliban in Buner stands outside her tent at the Yar Hussain relief camp in Chota Lahore, Swabi, Pakistan. Over 3 million people were believed to be displaced. More than 150,000 people forced to flee their homes in Swat, Buner and Lower Dir faced harsh living conditions in camps. 12th May 2009

First Prize: News Folio
Daniel Berehulak GETTY IMAGES

A Kashmiri girl is consoled as she mourns the death of teenager Zahid Farooq during his funeral on the outskirts of Srinagar, Kashmir, India. Over a thousand Kashmiris gathered to protest the death of the second teenager in a week. His relatives claim Farooq was shot dead by Indian security forces. 6th February 2010

Following spread
William Cherry PRESSEYE
Republican John Brady's mother Margaret and sister Lorna grieve at his coffin as an armed Real IRA guard of honour stands vigil. The Strabane Republican died whilst in PSNI custody at the city's Strand Road police station. 8th October 2009

Jeff J Mitchell GETTY IMAGES

Colleagues of firefighter Ewan Williamson gather in torrential rain outside St Giles Cathedral in Edinburgh. Firefighters from across the country paid their respects to Ewan Williamson who died while attending a fire at the Balmoral Bar 10 days earlier. 22nd July 2009

Steve Humphreys IRISH INDEPENDENT

Anthony McDonagh, left, and his son Eddie attend the funeral of their sons and brothers at Our Lady of Lourdes church in Drogheda. They were killed in a fatal fire at the family home. 23rd March 2009

Following spread
Adam Dean PANOS
US Army Soldiers from Viper Company 126, 1st Platoon relax outside the command centre at Restrepo Firebase in the restive Korengal Valley close to the Pakistan border in the Kunar Province of Afghanistan.
7th March 2009

First Prize: Photo Essay
Kieran Dodds PANOS
94 year old Golidem (94) holds her ID card in a small hut in rural Zimbabwe. 1st April 2009

First Prize: Photo Essay
Kieran Dodds PANOS
A seven-year old boy warms him self over some ashes. He is an orphan looked after by his 57 year old grandfather who works on a white owned farm near Bulawayo, Zimbabwe. 4th April 2009

First Prize: Photo Essay
Kieran Dodds PANOS
A new coalition government brings the hope of new life in Zimbabwe but the effects of mass inflation, hunger, disease and political violence remain. Minister of Education David Coltart of the MDC takes up office as part of the new government coalition under the gaze of Robert Mugabe who remains the President. 31st March 2009

First Prize: Photo Essay
Kieran Dodds PANOS
The family of an 18-year old cholera victim comfort one another following her death in a suburb of Harare. 31st March 2009

First Prize: Photo Essay
Kieran Dodds PANOS
Playing children reflected in raw sewage flowing down the streets of Bulawayo. Outbreaks of cholera are directly linked to effluent contamination of water supplies. Following thousands of deaths in the country over the last year, government and international groups are hopeful lessons have been learned and clean water will flow in the cities and towns this rainy season. 2nd April 2009

Following spread
First Prize: Photo Essay
Kieran Dodds PANOS
Elijah digs graves in a suburban cemetery of Harare, Zimbabwe. He complains of working barefoot next to the freshly buried cholera victims. Around 100,000 cholera cases were confirmed with over 4,000 deaths since August 2008. A crowd gathers in the distance for three simultaneous burials, one said to be an MDC supporter killed for their political allegiance. 31st March 2009

Adam Dean PANOS
Children aged 5 and 6 perform in a song and dance propaganda show at the Schoolchildren's Palace in Pyongyang, North Korea. 28th July 2009

Adam Dean PANOS
Young Koreans dance in front of the Juche tower in Pyongyang, North Korea. 27th July 2009

Adam Dean PANOS
Soldiers and civilians wait to board a train on the outskirts of Pyongyang, North Korea. 30th July 2009

Adam Dean PANOS
North Korean passengers ride on a train with portraits of Kim Il Sung and Kim Jong Il looking over them on the outskirts of Pyongyang. 30th July 2009

Adam Dean PANOS
A man rides on the back of a full tram in Pyongyang, North Korea. 29th July 2009

Following spread
Gareth Iwan Jones SWNS
An unidentified man in his fifties jumps to his death
from the Avonmouth Bridge on the M5 near Bristol.
The northbound lanes of the motorway were closed
causing 20 mile queues over the Bank Holiday weekend.
28th August 2009

David Azia
Steam locomotives operating within the open-cast coal mine in Zhalainuoer, Inner Mongolia, China.
24th March 2009

Jon Super
Smoke rises from Fiddlers Ferry Power Station, a coal fired power station located in Cheshire in the north-west of England. 16th February 2010

Cathal McNaughton REUTERS
Game hangs on a clothes line in preparation for being butchered in Garron Point, Co. Antrim, Northern Ireland.
18th January 2010

James Glossop THE TIMES
Crista Wilson plays on 'Earth Mounds', an installation by the artist Charles Jencks at Jupiter Artland, a small sculpture park on the outskirts of Edinburgh.
21st December 2009

Following spread
Sean Smith THE GUARDIAN
Village elders kneel to pray in a break during talks with soldiers of the US 501st Airborne Infantry after an IED had killed one man at Nasow Kheyl en route to Jani Kheyl in Afghanistan. 4th June 2009

54 year old Dada Mohammed Kehel — a Bedouin woman at her home in Tifariti, in Polisario controlled Western Sahara. 31st October 2009

Tuareg herdsman fight their way through sandstorms at Lake Banzena in Mali which has not seen rain for over 6 months. The most severe drought to hit the area in 29 years has devastated the key water source causing severe problems for the rare herd of 400 desert elephants who use the lake as their watering hole on the last leg of their migration route before the rains come. 5th May 2009

Dan Kitwood GETTY IMAGES

A group of San bushmen from the Khomani San community practice their hunter-gatherer craft in the Southern Kalahari desert, South Africa. One of the largest studies of African genetics by an international team from the University of Pennsylvania, published in April 2009, revealed that the San of Southern Africa are the most genetically diverse on earth, and that the San homeland could be the spot where modern humanity began. 15th October 2009

Dan Kitwood GETTY IMAGES

A San bushmen from the Khomani San community lights a fire in the Southern Kalahari desert.

16th October 2009

Dan Kitwood GETTY IMAGES

A bushman from the Khomani San community strikes a traditional pose in the Southern Kalahari desert.

16th October 2009

Andrew McConnell PANOS
A keyboard floats in a polluted lagoon at Agbogbloshie dump in Accra, Ghana. The suburb of Agbogbloshie has in recent years become a dumping ground for computers and electronic waste from Europe and the USA. Hundreds of tons of e-waste end up here every month as countries in the West attempt to unload their ever increasing stockpiles of toxic junk. 16th March 2009

Andrew McConnell PANOS
Computer hard drives are stacked high at an importers warehouse in Accra, Ghana. The majority of them are not working and will be scrapped. Containers arriving in Ghana with computers are often labelled 'second hand goods' to bypass international laws. In reality as much as 80% of the equipment will be obsolete or broken.
18th March 2009

Andrew McConnell PANOS
Goats are herded around Agbogbloshie dump while smoke rises from burning e-waste in Accra, Ghana.
16th March 2009

Carl de Souza AGENCE FRANCE PRESSE
Austrian artist Willi Dorner's 'Bodies in Spaces'
performing arts troupe assume positions in awkward
spaces on an hour long route through London toured
by members of the public. 16th October 2009

Jason Alden
A competitor takes part in the Barclaycard World
Freerun Championships in Trafalgar Square, London.
15th August 2009

Following spread
Jason Hawkes
The City of London at dusk. 26th October 2009

David Levene
A pedestrian scramble at Shibuya intersection in
Tokyo, which is said to be the busiest in the world
with many hundreds of people crossing every few
minutes. 7th April 2009

Dan Kitwood GETTY IMAGES
A worker uses the lift on the Lloyd's Insurance building
in London. Alistair Darling announced that new laws
were to be brought in to ensure banking bonuses were
to be granted on a performance basis rather than be
given automatically. 28th September 2010

First Prize: Royalty and Entertainment
Mark Stewart
Prince William looks at his Grandmother's throne
before making a speech at the Australia Day reception
at Government House in Melbourne, Australia.
21st January 2010

Steve Parsons PRESS ASSOCIATION
Baroness Thatcher at the opening of the new wing at Canine Partners National Training Centre in Heyshott, West Sussex. 2nd June 2009

Chris Jackson GETTY IMAGES
Camilla, Duchess of Cornwall holds up a bag she was given as a gift after a visit to the 999 club in Deptford, south east London. The 999 Club offers help and support to the community allowing the homeless to sleep, rest and eat free food. 10th September 2009

Following spread
Julien Behal PRESS ASSOCIATION
Queen Elizabeth II signs the visitors' book during a visit
to Lisneal College in Co. Derry at the start of three day
tour of Northern Ireland. 6th May 2009

Date   Name   Address

Date

Andy Hooper DAILY MAIL
Sprinter Dwain Chambers reflects on his life as he sits
in the back garden of his house in Enfield, London.
26th February 2009

Charles McQuillan PACEMAKER PRESS
An Orangeman listens to the address at the
Independents Orange Parade in Rasharkin,
Northern Ireland. 13th July 2009

Following spread
Brad Wakefield SWNS
Lady GaGa performs at the Glastonbury Festival, in
Somerset on The Other Stage. 26th June 2009

Following spread
Anthony Devlin PRESS ASSOCIATION
Maximo Park performing during the 2009 Glastonbury
Festival at Worthy Farm in Pilton, Somerset. 27th June 2009

Leon Neal AGENCE FRANCE PRESSE
Punk pioneer Iggy Pop poses with his 'Living Legend'
award in London's Dorchester Hotel after the 5th
annual Marshall Classic Rock Roll of Honour Awards.
1st November 2009

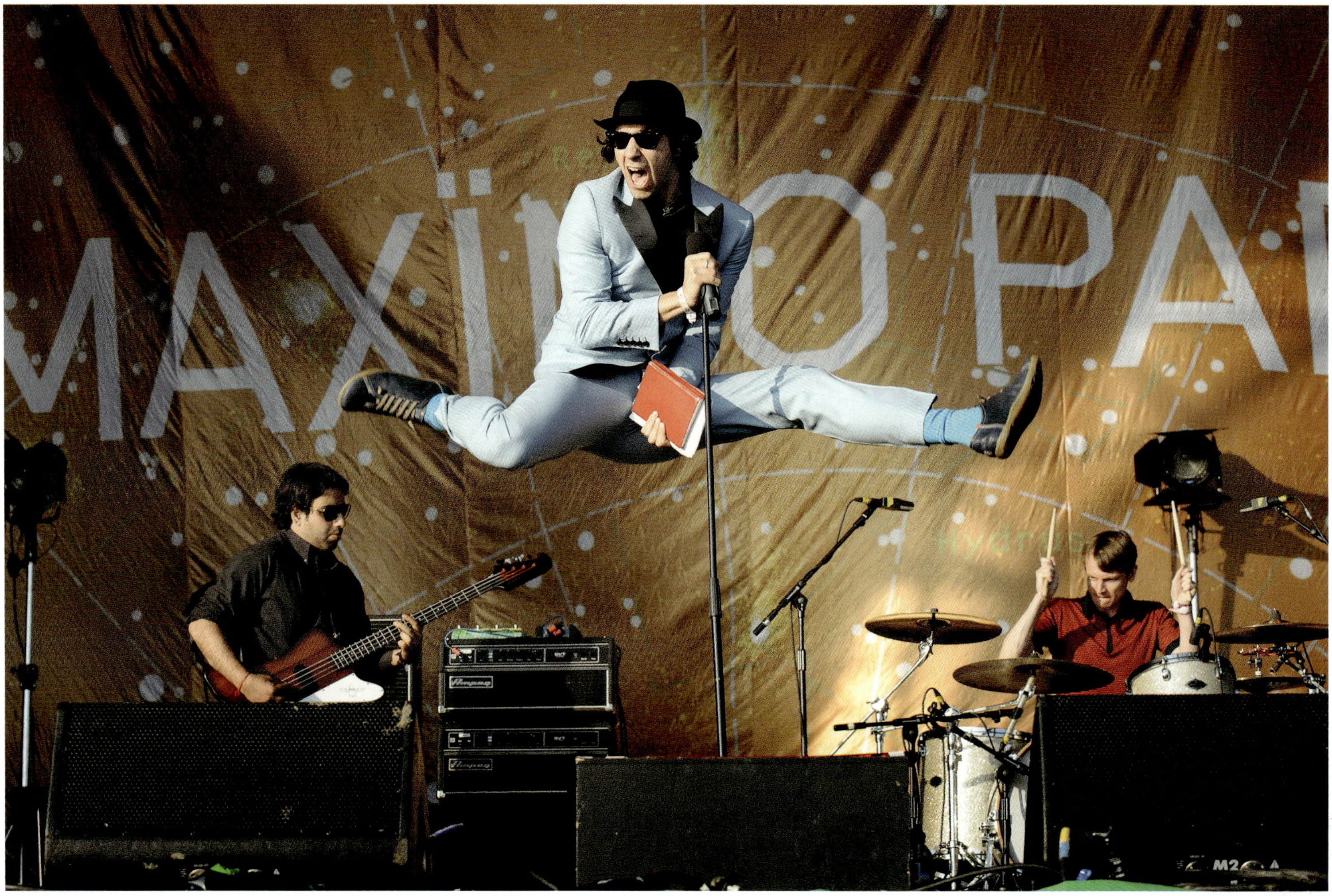
MAXÏ
O PA

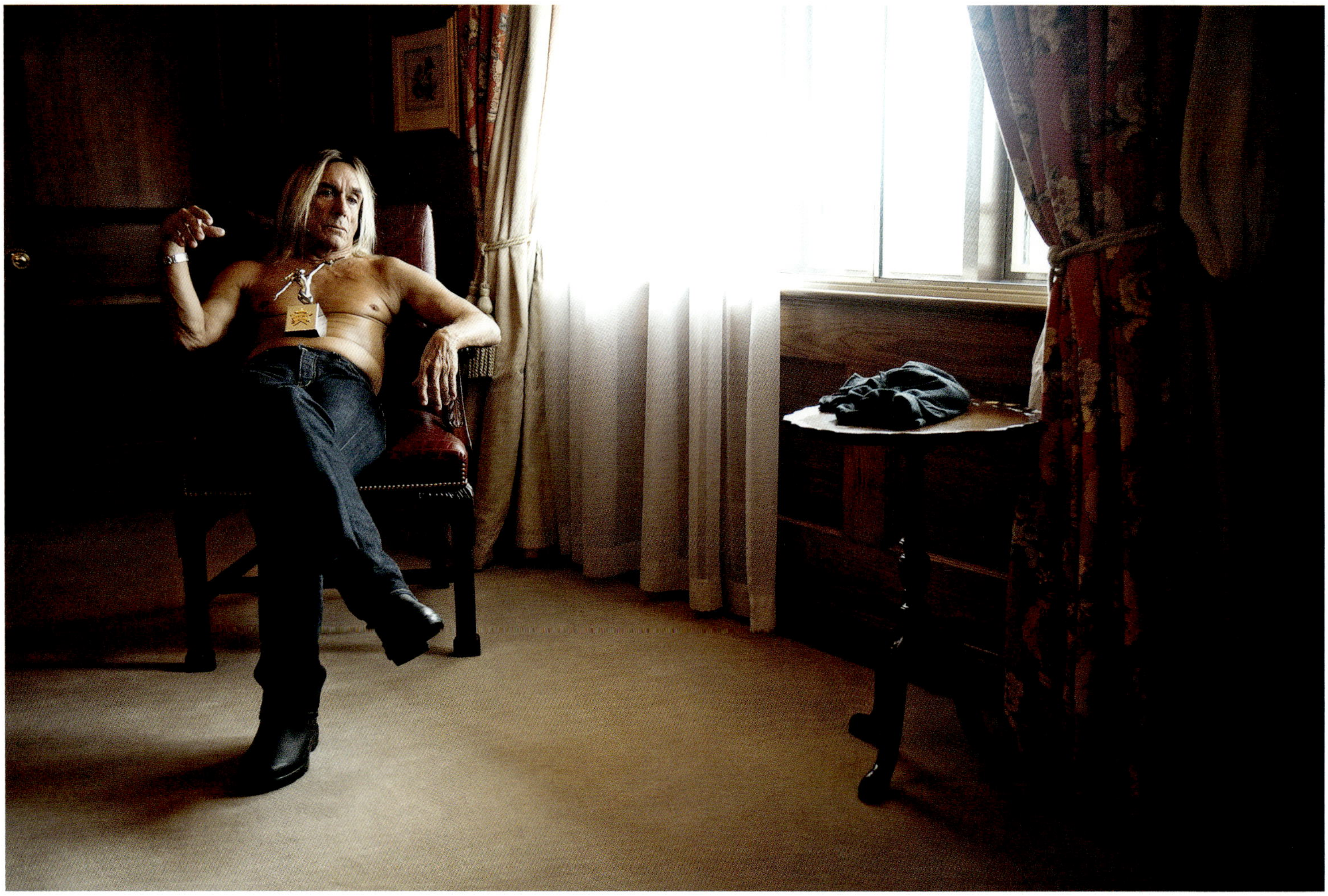

Charles McQuillan PACEMAKER PRESS

A loyalist youth sports a black eye as he stands watch on south Belfast's Sandy Row as final preperations are made for the 12th of July bonfire celebrations.
11th July 2009

Brian David Stevens

Dubstep musican EL-B (real name Lewis Beadle) is a British electronic music producer who produces mainly hip hop and UK garage. He is also noted as a pioneer of the dubstep genre. He runs the Ghost Recordings label and is also part of the duo El-Tuff and the band Groove Chronicles, London. 12th September 2009

Steve Humphreys IRISH INDEPENDENT
A press briefing outside Hillsborough Castle in Northern Ireland after the murders of a Police Officer and two soldiers threatened to destablise the peace process with Minister for Justice Dermot Ahern, Minister for Foriegn Affairs Micheal Martin, Sean Woodward Secretary of State for Northern Ireland and Paul Goggins Northern Ireland Security Minister. 10th March 2009

Warren Allott
Lord Goldsmith leaves the Iraq Inquiry after giving evidence on the legality of the Iraq War. In 2003 Lord Goldsmith wrote a nine paragraph legal opinion claiming the invasion of Iraq was legal and it was this legal advice to the Blair Government which led to the invasion of Iraq. 27th January 2010

Magnus Andersson
Mayor of London Boris Johnson falls in the water as he takes part in a community clean up of the Ravensbourne river in Bellingham, Kent. Debbie Leach, chief executive of Thames21, comes to his rescue. 4th June 2009

Richard Pohle THE TIMES
BNP leader Nick Griffin is bundled away by bodyguards after he was attacked outside Parliament by anti-nazi demonstrators, London. 9th June 2009

Eddie Mulholland DAILY TELEGRAPH
US President Barack Obama and The Prime Minister Gordon Brown return to Downing Street where The President shakes hands with PC Michael Zamora on the steps of No 10. 1st April 2009

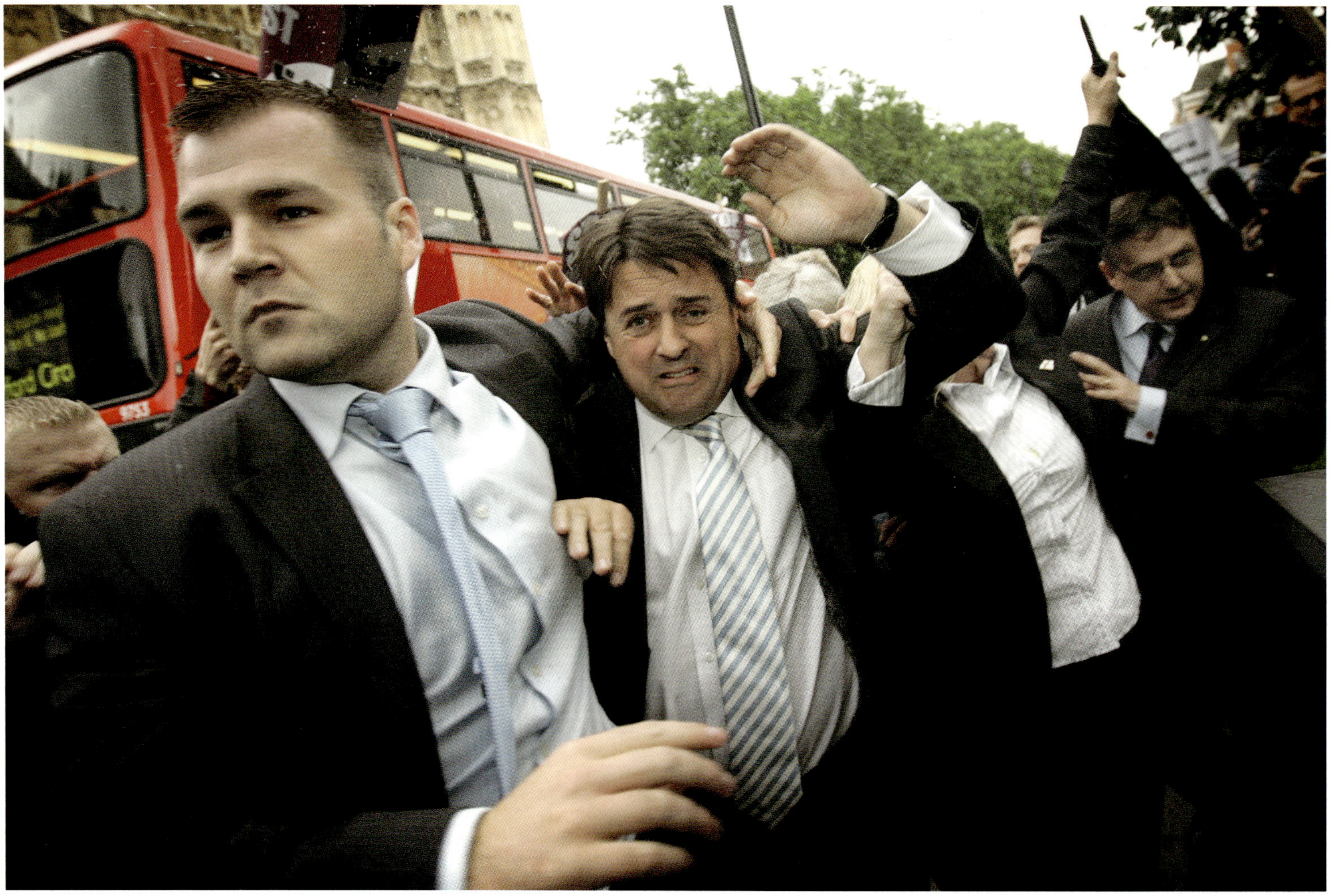

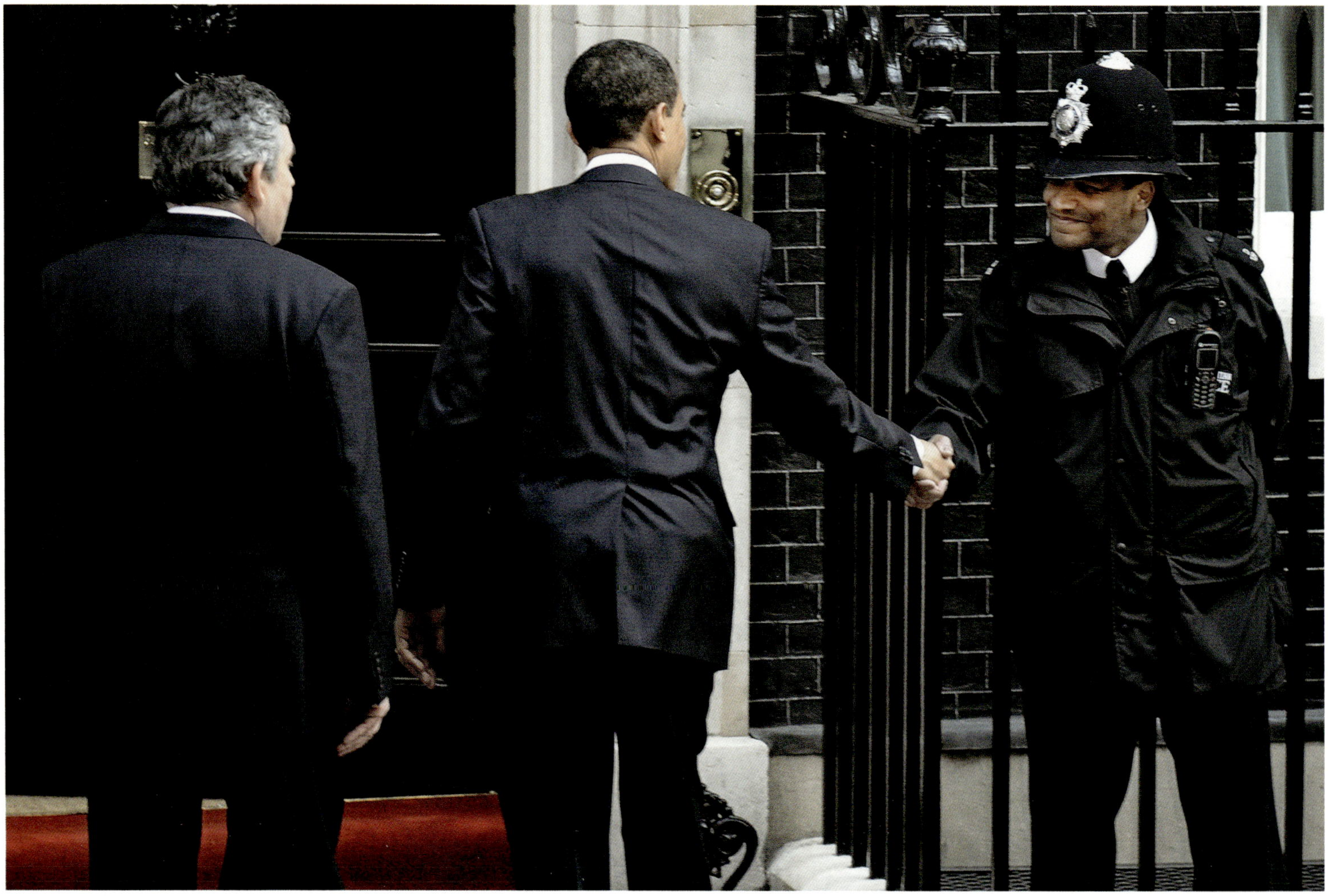

First Prize: Portraits
Cathal McNaughton
Irish Snooker Legend Alex Higgins pictured in
Palmerstown House, County Kildare, Ireland.
2nd January 2010

Following spread
Tom Pilston
Actor Clive Owen, London. 11th March 2009

John Giles PRESS ASSOCIATION
Prime Minister Gordon Brown shows the strain of a
difficult week as he visits Bradford, West Yorkshire.
8th May 2009

Following spread
Lefteris Pitarakis AP
Lance Corporal Stephen Heeley poses for pictures with
his horse Yeoman during rehearsals for the Windsor
Castle Royal Tattoo at Windsor Castle, Berkshire.
29th April 2009

David Bebber THE TIMES
4 year old Akisa who fled fighting between Houthi
militants and government forces stands outside a
UNHCR tent in a refugee camp near the town of Hadja
in north west Yemen. 3rd October 2010

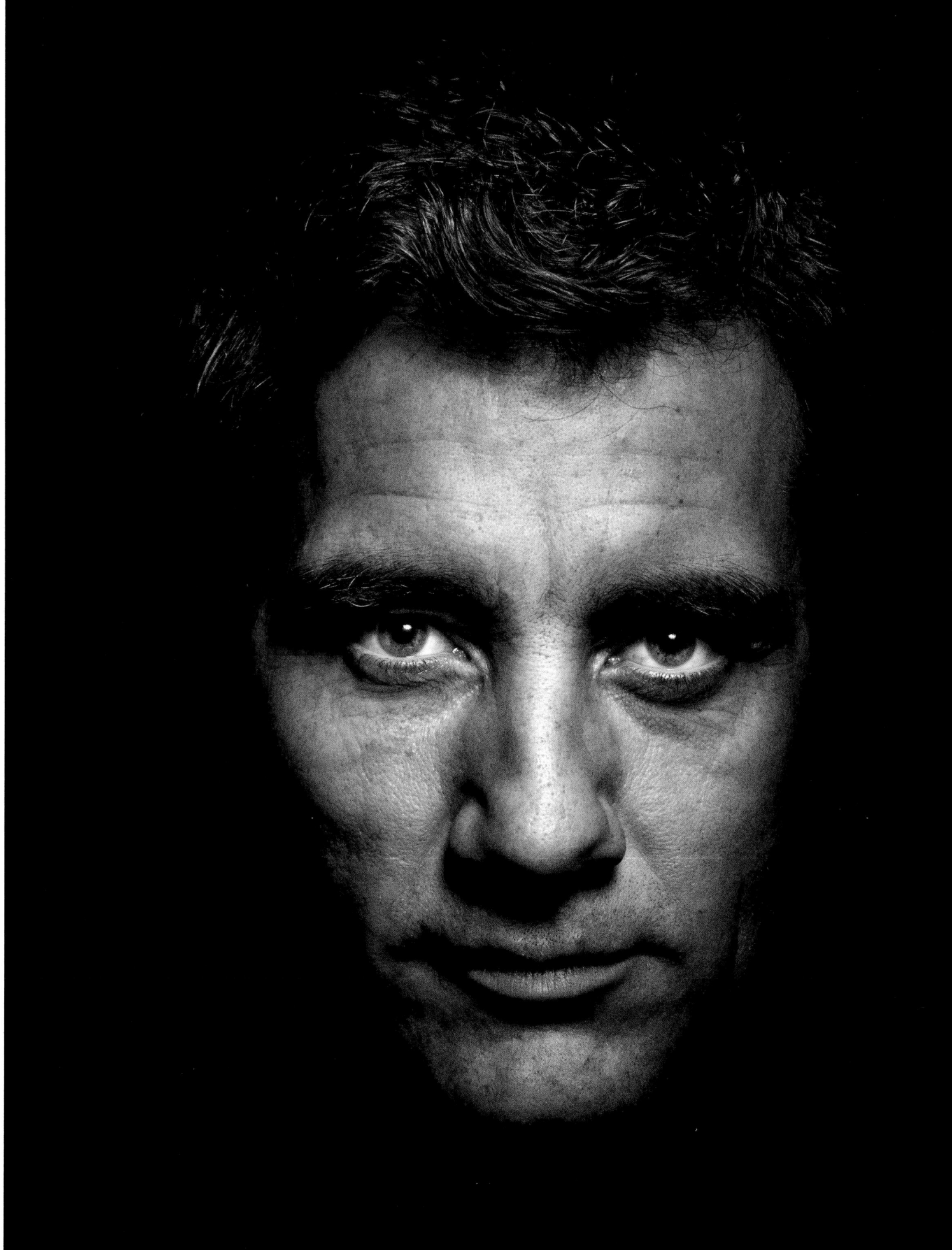

Julien Behal PRESS ASSOCIATION
Danny Balan lifts up the waxwork head of Pope John
Paul II into place beside the waxwork of current Pope
Pope Benedict XVI as final preparations are made
for the official opening of the re-opened National
Wax Museum Plus in Foster Place, Dublin, Ireland.
7th October 2009

Luke MacGregor REUTERS
A couple pause among crosses and poppies in the Field
of Remembrance in the grounds of Westminster Abbey,
London. 7th November 2009

Following spread
First Prize: The Arts
Oli Scarff GETTY IMAGES
Sky television film a performance of Swan Lake by the
English National Ballet in 3D in The Painted Hall of the
Old Royal Naval College in Greenwich. 9th April 2009

Following spread
Jess Hurd REPORTDIGITAL.CO.UK
Toy Graveyard, Normandy. France. 16th October 2009

91

Daniel Berehulak GETTY IMAGES
A Hindu priest tosses coloured powder known as Gulal,
passing the blessings of Lord Krishna to Hindu devotees
as they play with colour during Holi celebrations at the
Bankey Bihari Temple in Vrindavan, India. 26th February 2010

Matt Cardy GETTY IMAGES
Stars in the night sky rotate above the distinctive
chimney stack on the top of Cape Cornwall near
St Just, England. 12th April 2009

Dan Kitwood GETTY IMAGES

A deer stands in the snow in Richmond Park, Surrey.
16th December 2009

Ian MacNicol

Hamish a Cocker spaniel belonging to gamekeeper
Graham White bounds though the snow near his home
on the Holylee Estate in Peeblesshire. 30th November 2009

Following spread
Bradley Ormesher THE TIMES
Mr G Gallagher takes a tumble off De Luain Gorm at
The Chair in the John Smith Fox Hunters Steeple Chase
at Aintree, near Liverpool. 3rd April 2009

First Prize: Sports Folio
Laurence Griffiths GETTY IMAGES
Graeme Swann of Nottinghamshire and England
poses for portraits at Trent Bridge in Nottingham.
8th January 2009

Following spread
First Prize: Sports Action
Gareth Copley PRESS ASSOCIATION
England's Jonathan Trott is run out by Australia's Simon
Katich during the fifth npower Test Match at The Oval,
London. 26th May 2009

First Prize: Sports Specialist Folio
Clive Mason GETTY IMAGES
Heikki Kovalainen of Finland and McLaren Mercedes
drives during qualifying for the Singapore Formula
One Grand Prix at the Marina Bay Street Circuit.
26th September 2009

First Prize: Sports Specialist Folio
Clive Mason GETTY IMAGES
Sebastian Vettel of Germany and Red Bull Racing drives
on his way to winning the Chinese Formula One Grand
Prix at the Shanghai International Circuit. 19th April 2009

First Prize: Sports Specialist Folio
Clive Mason GETTY IMAGES
Jenson Button of Great Britain and Brawn GP drives
during the Abu Dhabi Formula One Grand Prix at the
Yas Marina Circuit. 1st November 2009

Amy Williams of Great Britain and Northern Ireland
celebrates with the Union Jack after she won the Gold
Medal in the women's skeleton on day 8 of the 2010
Vancouver Winter Olympics at the Whistler Sliding
Centre. 19th February 2010

First Prize: Sports Specialist Folio
Jenson Button of Great Britain and Brawn GP celebrates
after winning the Australian Formula One Grand Prix at
the Albert Park Circuit in Melbourne. 29th March 2009

First Prize: Sports Folio
Laurence Griffiths GETTY IMAGES
Barcelona fans during the UEFA Super Cup Final
between FC Barcelona and Shakhtar Donetsk at
The Stade Louis II Stadium in Monaco. 28th August 2009

Clive Rose GETTY IMAGES
Alexandre Despatie of Canada competes in the mens
3m springboard final during the 13th FINA World
Championships at Stadio del Nuoto in Rome, Italy.
23rd July 2009

Following spread
First Prize: Winter Olympic Singles
Clive Rose GETTY IMAGES
Stefan Georgiev of Bulgaria competes during the Alpine
Skiing Men's Super Combined Downhill on day 10 of the
Vancouver 2010 Winter Olympics at Whistler Creekside
in Canada. 21st February 2010

First Prize: Sports Folio
Laurence Griffiths   GETTY IMAGES
Sir Alex Ferguson of Manchester United walks out
during the Barclays Premier League match between
Aston Villa and Manchester United at Villa Park in
Birmingham. 10th February 2010

Javier Garcia
Nicolas Anelka of Chelsea stands in the pouring rain
during the Champion's League game against Porto at
Stamford Bridge. 15th September 2009

First Prize: Sports Folio
Laurence Griffiths GETTY IMAGES
Arsenal Manager Arsene Wenger gestures after being sent to the stands during the Barclays Premier League match between Manchester United and Arsenal at Old Trafford. 29th August 2009

First Prize: Sports Folio
Laurence Griffiths GETTY IMAGES
Brad Thorn of New Zealand breaks past Matthew Rees and Martin Roberts of Wales during the Invesco Perpetual Series Match between Wales and New Zealand at The Millennium Stadium in Cardiff.
7th November 2009

Following spread
First Prize: Sports Features
Sean Smith THE GUARDIAN
All Star Wrestling at Birkenhead on Merseyside.
25th November 2009

The Entrants for 2010

Bruce Adams
Marcos Agrelli
Jason Alden
Matthew Alexander
Esme Allen
Carol Allen Storey
Warren Allott
Euan Anderson
Brian Anderson
Magnus Andersson
John Angerson
Facundo Arrizabalaga
Marc Aspland
David Azia
Steve Back
Andrew Baker
Roger Bamber
Fraser Band
Howard Barlow
Jane Barlow
Tony Bartholomew
David Bebber
Ben Begley
Julien Behal
Callum Bennetts
Steve Bent
Daniel Berehulak
Charlie Bibby
Jon Bond
Christopher Booth
Harry Borden
Stuart Boulton
Andrew Boyers
James Breeden
Philip Brown
Simon Brown
Sarah Lucy Brown
Henry Browne
Gary Browne
Mikael Buck
Jason Bye
Jason Cairnduff
Andre Camara
Richard Cannon

Matt Cardy
Niall Carson
Gareth Cattermole
Graham Chadwick
Richard Chambury
Gareth Chaney
Paul Chappells
William Cherry
Bethany Clarke
C J Clarke
Felix Clay
Tal Cohen
Blake-Ezra Cole
Katie Collins
Mark Condren
Len Copland
Gareth Copley
Glenn Copus
Vicki Couchman
Andy Couldridge
Carl Court
Andrew Cowie
Steve Cox
Aidan Crawley
Shaun Curry
Simon Dack
Brian David Stevens
Alan Davidson
Simon Dawson
Mike Day
Fabio De Paola
Carl de Souza
Adam Dean
Peter Dench
Adrian Dennis
Anthony Devlin
Nigel Dickinson
Kieran Dodds
Kieran Doherty
Andrew Duke
Matt Dunham
Michael Dunlea
Hazel Dunlop
Mike Egerton

Paul Ellis
Stuart Emmerson
Jon Enoch
Steve Etherington
John Ferguson
Rick Findler
Julian Finney
Ian Forsyth
Stuart Freedman
Sam Frost
Gareth Fuller
Sam Furlong
Chris Furlong
Kieran Glavin
Andy Garbutt
Javier Garcia
Adam Gasson
Clive Gee
John Giles
Paul Gilham
Paul Glendell
James Glossop
Martin Godwin
Anna Gordon
Rowan Griffiths
Spencer Griffiths
Laurence Griffiths
Ben Gurr
Simon Hadley
Andy Hall
Pal Hansen
Paul Harding
Rebecca Harley
Terry Harris
Brian Harris
Graham Harrison
Rupert Hartley
Jason Hawkes
Richard Heathcote
Scott Heavey
Rune Hellestad
Mike Hewitt
Steve Hill
Jack Hill
Nigel Hillier
Neil Hodge
David Hoffman
David Hogan
Ian Homer
Andy Hooper
Scott Hornby
Alexander Hug
Simon Hulme
Steve Humphreys
Richard Humphries
Jess Hurd
Samir Hussein
Tim Ireland
Susannah Ireland

Catherine Ivill
Christopher Jackson
Robert Johns
Gareth Iwan Jones
Robin Jones
Peter Jordan
Nils Jorgensen
Frantzesco Kangaris
Liz Kearsley
Eddie Keogh
Ady Kerry
Ross Kinnaird
Glyn Kirk
Matthew Kirwan
Dan Kitwood
Ash Knotek
Sarah Lee
Colm Lenaghan
David Levene
John Linton
Dominic Lipinski
Warren Little
Alex Livesey
Matthew Lloyd
Ian Longthorne
Lawrence Looi
Mikal Ludlow
Michael Lusmore
Lawrence Lustig
Peter Macdiarmid
Luke MacGregor
Ian MacNicol
Thomas Main
Mark Makela
Dylan Martinez
Clive Mason
Dan Matthams
Paul Mattsson
Liam McBurney
Andrew McConnell
John D McHugh
John Mcintyre
Rebecca Mckevitt
Cathal McNaughton
Colin McPherson
Charles McQuillan
Mary Mehrmand
Toby Melville
Sebastian Meyer
Dustin Michailovs
Andrew Milligan
Jane Mingay
Jeff Mitchell
Clara Molden
Mimi Mollica
Jeff Moore
Brendan Moran
Peter Muhly
Eddie Mulholland

Rebecca Naden
Leon Neal
Peter Nicholls
Ian Nicholson
Phil Noble
Bryan O'Brien
Jason O'Brien
Heathcliff O'Malley
Bradley Ormesher
Jeff Overs
Chryssa Panoussiadou
Dave Parker
David Parry
Steve Parsons
Richard Pelham
Teri Pengilley
Gary Perkin
Tom Pilston
Lefteris Pitarakis
Christopher Pledger
Suzanne Plunkett
Richard Pohle
Stephen Pond
Nick Ponty
Jonathan Porter
Geoff Pugh
Ben Radford
Lucy Ray
Mark Readman
Carl Recine
Michael Regan
Martin Rickett
Vaughn Ridley
Lorna Roach
Graeme Robertson
Ian Robinson
Geoff Robinson
Nigel Roddis
Paul Rogers
Clive Rose
Peter Sandground
David Sandison
Oli Scarff
Rii Schroer
Jeremy Selwyn
Dwayne Senior
Stephen Shepherd
Martin Shields
Dave Shopland
John Sibley
Derek Simpson
Stephen Simpson
Jamie Simpson
Christian Sinibaldi
Guy Smallman
Tim Smith
Sean Smith
Jeff Spicer
Matt Sprake

Tina Stallard
Darren Staples
Mark Stewart
Akira Suemori
Jonathan Super
Justin Sutcliffe
Jeremy Sutton-Hibbert
Reuben Tabner
Justin Tallis
Sang Tan
Ray Tang
Jason Tanner
Peter Tarry
Edmond Terakopian
Andrew Testa
Micha Theiner
Paul Thomas
Mark Thompson
Lee Thompson
Dave Thompson
Chris Tofalos
Abbie Trayler-Smith
Morgan Treacy
Felipe Trueba Garcia
Mary Turner
Carmen Valino
Yvonne Vaughan
James Veysey
Bruno Vincent
Richard Wainwright
Brad Wakefield
Stuart Walker
Eamon Ward
Dave Warren
Zak Waters
Mark Waugh
Anna Weaver
Andy Weekes
Stefan Wermuth
James Whitaker
David White
Emily Whitfield-Wicks
Lewis Whyld
Kirsty Wigglesworth
Jim Wileman
Sarah Williams
Les Wilson
William Wintercross
Matt Writtle
Andrew Yates

09

Bruce Adams
Jason Alden
Matthew Alexander
Carol Allen Storey
Warren Allott
Brian Anderson
Magnus Andersson
Julian Andrews
Frederic Aranda
Facundo Arrizabalaga
Matthew Ashton
Marc Aspland
David Azia
Steve Back
Stephen Bagness
Andrew Baker
Roger Bamber
Fraser Band
Jane Barlow
Tony Bartholomew
David Bebber
Ben Begley
Julien Behal
Guy Bell
Callum Bennetts
Daniel Berehulak
Andy Blackmore
James Boardman
Jon Bond
Christopher Booth
Harry Borden
Shaun Botterill
Stuart Boulton
Philip Brown
Sarah Lucy Brown
Mark Bullimore
Richard Cannon
Matt Cardy
Angela Catlin
Gareth Cattermole
Graham Chadwick
Darren Chaplin
Paul Chappells
Wattie Cheung

Yasuyohi Chiba
Daniel Chung
Nobby Clark
C J Clarke
Felix Clay
Philip Coburn
Tal Cohen
Phil Cole
Katie Collins
Stuart Conway
Gareth Copley
Vicki Couchman
Carl Court
Christopher Cox
Alexander Craig
Shaun Curry
Simon Dack
Sanjit Das
Brian David Stevens
Adam Davy
Jason Dawson
Simon Dawson
Fabio De Paola
Carl de Souza
Adam Dean
Sean Dempsey
Peter Dench
Euan Denholm
Adrian Dennis
Anthony Devlin
Nigel Dickinson
Kieran Dodds
Kieran Doherty
Matt Dunham
Michael Dunlea
Hazel Dunlop
Nic Dunlop
Jim Dyson
Mike Egerton
Stuart Emmerson
Rick Findler
Julian Finney
Adrian Fisk
Ian Forsyth

Andrew Fox
Gareth Fuller
Sam Furlong
Chris Furlong
Yoav Galai
James Galloway
Kieran Galvin
Andy Garbutt
Javier Garcia
Adam Gasson
Clive Gee
John Giles
Paul Gilham
Cate Gillon
James Glossop
Martin Godwin
Anna Gordon
Laurence Griffiths
Stuart Griffiths
Spencer Griffiths
Ben Gurr
Andy Hall
Rosie Hallam
Pal Hansen
Paul Harding
Richard Harris
Stuart Harrison
Mark Harrison
Graham Harrison
Jason Hawkes
Richard Heathcote
Scott Heavey
Rune Hellestad
Maros Herc
Tom Hevezi
Mike Hewitt
Andrew Higgins
Jack Hill
Stephen Hird
Neil Hodge
David Hoffman
Jim Holden
Andy Hooper
James Horan
Scott Hornby
Alexander Hug
Richard Humphries
Jess Hurd
Susannah Ireland
Tim Ireland
Christopher Ison
Christopher Jackson
James O Jenkins
Tom Jenkins
Robert Johns
Gareth Jones
Ian Jones
Dan Jones
Nils Jorgensen

Irina Kalashnikova
Frantzesco Kangaris
Liz Kearsley
Findlay Kember
Clare Kendall
Dan Kennedy
Eddie Keogh
Ady Kerry
Ross Kinnaird
Glyn Kirk
Matthew Kirwan
Dan Kitwood
David Klein
Will Leach
Colm Lenaghan
Bryn Lennon
Amit Lennon
David Levene
Geraint Lewis
Dominic Lipinski
Warren Little
Alex Livesey
Matthew Lloyd
Mikal Ludlow
Michael Lusmore
Lawrence Lustig
Daniel Lynch
Peter Macdiarmid
Ian MacNicol
Toby Madden
Thomas Main
Mark Makela
Mike Marsland
Dylan Martinez
Clive Mason
Dan Matthams
James McCauley
Andrew McConnell
Damien Mcfadden
John D McHugh
Kieran McManus
Cathal McNaughton
Colin McPherson
Charles McQuillan
Colin Mearns
Toby Melville
Andrew Meredith
Dustin Michailovs
Stuart Miller
Andrew Milligan
Jane Mingay
Jeff J Mitchell
Clara Molden
Brendan Moran
Peter Muhly
Eddie Mulholland
Max Nash
Leon Neal
Paul Nicholls

Ian Nicholson
Phil Noble
Linda Nylind
Jason O'Brien
Tony O'Brien
Bryan O'Brien
Jeff Overs
Dave Parker
David Parry
Steve Parsons
Andrew Parsons
Richard Pelham
Teri Pengilley
Dan Phillips
Hugo Philpott
Ryan Pierse
Tom Pilston
Mark Pinder
Lefteris Pitarakis
Jonathan Player
Christopher Pledger
Suzanne Plunkett
Richard Pohle
Stephen Pond
Jonathan Porter
Geoff Pugh
Simon Rawles
Nick Ray
Lucy Ray
Mark Readman
Carl Recine
Michael Regan
Kiran Ridley
Steve Roberts
Graeme Robertson
Mark Robinson
Nigel Roddis
Clive Rose
Stefan Rousseau
Peter Sandground
David Sandison
Oli Scarff
Georgie Scott
Jeremy Selwyn
Dwayne Senior
Ahikam Seri
Mark Sheldon
Stephen Shepherd
Martin Shields
Dave Shopland
Jonathan Short
John Sibley
Julian Simmonds
Derek Simpson
Jamie Simpson
Christian Sinibaldi
David Sleator
Guy Smallman
Sean Smith

Tim Smith
Bill Smyth
Matt Sprake
Simon Stacpoole
Tina Stallard
Michael Steele
Mark Stewart
Tom Stoddart
Helen Stone
Bettina Strenske
Akira Suemori
Jonathan Super
Justin Sutcliffe
Sang Tan
Ray Tang
Edmond Terakopian
Andrew Testa
Micha Theiner
Mark Thompson
Dave Thompson
Lee Thompson
Ed Thompson
Allan Titmuss
Dan Towers
Abbie Trayler-Smith
Morgan Treacy
Graham Trott
Felipe Trueba Garcia
Ant Upton
Toby Vandevelde
James Veysey
Rui Vieira
Bruno Vincent
Richard Wainwright
Brad Wakefield
Stuart Walker
Eamon Ward
Dave Warren
Jonathan Warren
Zak Waters
Mark Waugh
Toby Weller
Haydn West
David White
Lewis Whyld
Kirsty Wigglesworth
Phil Wilkinson
Keith Williams
Sarah Williams
Les Wilson
Rosie Windsor
William Wintercross
Matt Writtle
Andrew Yates
Sandy Young
Ronen Zvulun